Constitutional Developments of the Habsburg Empire in the Last Decades before its Fall

Constitutional Developments of the Habsburg Empire in the Last Decades before its Fall

The Materials of Polish-Hungarian Conference

Cracow, September 2007

Edited by Kazimierz Baran

Jagiellonian University Press

The publication of this volume was supported by the Jagiellonian University
– Departament of History of State and Law (research support funds)

COVER DESIGNER

Paweł Bigos

ISBN 978-83-233-2898-8

www.wuj.pl

Jagiellonian University Press
Editorial Offices: ul. Michałowskiego 9/2, 31-126 Kraków
Phone: 12-631-18-81, 12-631-18-82, Fax: 12-631-18-83
Distribution: Phone: 12-631-01-97, Phone/Fax: 12-631-01-98
Cell Phone: 0506-006-674, e-mail: sprzedaz@wuj.pl
Bank: PEKAO SA, nr 80 1240 4722 1111 0000 4856 3325

Contents

From the Editor of the Volume

The present volume contains a series of articles that make up the aftermatch of the Polish-Hungarian Conference on legal history that was held in Cracow, 23–24 September 2007. The Conference was devoted to the constitutional developments in the Habsburg monarchy in the last decades before its fall. In the reports that were delivered on this occasion a strong emphasis was laid on the constitutional liberalism characteristic of the Austro-Hungarian empire, and consequently – of the elements of *Rechtsstaat* detectable in this organism.

The readers of the present volume may find a considerable range of problems discussed in the respective papers. Thus the article by István Kajtár depicts the silhouette of Andor Csizmadia, an outstanding legal historian whose research was, to a large extent, devoted to the constitutional evolution of the Habsburg empire in the era of dualism that followed 1867. The papers by Krisztina Korsósné and Andrzej Dziadzio focus, in their turn, on the description of the symptoms of *Rechtsstaat* in the judiciary both in the Hungarian and the Austrian parts of the monarchy. An interesting image of relationships between State and Church in the Hungarian part of the dualistic state is presented in the article written by Eszter Herger. Zsuzsanna Peres, in her turn, explores in her paper the succession law of the epoch, and in that context analyses the instrument of *fideicomissum* and its contribution to the survival of Hungarian national heritage. A few articles of the volume may be qualified as *Polonica* since Polish issues are pushed to the foreground in them. Thus the article by Kazimierz Baran discusses the intrinsic game that Józef Piłsudski played with Austria which was the most liberal partitioner at that time, the game being designed to restore Poland's independent statehood. The paper by Grzegorz Kowalski, in its turn, demonstrates the large proportion of emigration liberty conferred on the inhabitants of Galicia and derived from the guaranties provided for by the December Constitution. The rustical relationships resembling those of serfdom and detectable in the Polish part of Spisz after the end of World War I are the subject-matter of the article by Władysław Pęksa. These relationships were reminiscent of the lord-peasant relationships that could be previously found in some areas of the Hungarian part of the Habsburg monarchy. And eventually the paper by Marian Małecki makes up an interesting contribution to the question of vitality of the royalistic constitutional concept as a possible option for Poland upon the end of World War I.

KAZIMIERZ BARAN

Józef Piłsudski's Attitude toward the Cause of Austria and Germany in World War I

1. Introductory Remarks. Józef Piłsudski: the Statesman of the Time of the War and of the Inter-war Period

Józef Piłsudski (1867–1935) was a particularly eminent statesman and a man of the military, remarkably anxious for restoring Poland's independence during World War I. In the inter-war time he also played a significant role in the Polish political life. In the early stage of his activities he tried to combine the socialist ideas with those whose objective was the restoring of independent statehood of his motherland. The sources confirm that before the outbreak of World War I he had a particularly accurate vision of future developments. He prophesied the disintegration of the three empires that at one time partitioned Poland. Therefore he thought it indispensable to form some nucleus of the future Polish army capable of defending the restored country in the environment that was hostile to it.

When the war broke out he had his share in forming the Polish legions which, while siding Austria, were involved in fighting against one partitioner: Russia. Apart from these activities, he as early as 1914, was busy preparing the clandestine troops composed of militarily trained men who, particularly on the area from which Russians were driven away, would make up a conspiratorial army. This secret army was referred to as the POW (*Polska Organizacja Wojskowa*). That army, he thought, would be needed when, as a result of further developments, the Poles would have to drop the cooperation with the Central Powers (Austria and Germany). The latter, while replacing Russians on the historically Polish territory, would consequently turn into the new occupiers thereof. From the point of view of the Poles the complete success of Germany and Austria was as undesirable as the success of Russia.

No wonder, therefore, that when in 1917 the question of independent Poland assumed the international dimension and began to be supported by eminent politicians of international scene Piłsudski and a large portion of his soldiers renounced their allegiance to the Austrian and German Emperors. This led to their internment and, sometimes, imprisonment.

Due to his persistent attempts at restoring Poland's independence and due to his conspiratorial experience Piłsudski grew into a charismatic personality. Out of his legionaries and the members of the POW there grew the millieu of so called *Piłsudski-ties* who later supported their leader in the inter-war period.[1]

Upon the end of World War I Piłsudski, as a symbol of struggle for independence, became fully involved in laying the foundations of the freshly regained independent state structures. When, however, in 1921 the Constitution of the Second Republic of Poland was adopted, he resigned from compeating for the position of the president since he believed that the scope of power vested in this office was unreasonably limited and boiled down to only representative functions. In fact the Constitution vested particular power in the lower house of the legislative body at the expense of competence of the upper house (the Senate) and the head of the State. This doubtless threatened the stability of future governmental Cabinets.

The Constitution introduced a typical parliamentary system based on the separation of powers and political responsibility of government to parliament. The Cabinets were formed by the winning party or the coalition of parties that could secure the support of parliamentary majority. The loss of support might result in the adoption by the lower house of the vote of no confidence vis-à-vis the Cabinet whose members would have to resign their posts. The point was, however, that in the 1921 system the President had only an illusionary power to dissolve the houses of parliament, he had also no right to initiate legislation, although these were the prerogatives that were usually awarded to the head of the State in the parliamentary system.

At that time for a few years Piłsudski disappeared from the political scene but simultaneously he tried to consolidate around himself the millieu of the former legionaries and the POW members as well as other groupings of symphatizers.

In the early 1920s Poland went through difficult days. The previous markets functioning during the partitions were disrupted. The Russian market was closed to Polish products. The country faced the runaway inflation and a lot of hostility as demonstrated by its neighbours: Weimar Republic of Germany and the Soviet Russia. Germany produced difficulties in Poland's access to the Baltic through the Free City of Gdańsk, and in 1925 it declared a kind of tarrif war on Poland, trying to weaken her economy. Poland, with enormous effort, tried to surmount these impediments. The Poles built a new seaport in Gdynia, balanced the budget and tried to develop the previously neglected lines of industry in chemistry and electrical engineering in order to become independent of their powerful western neighbour.[2]

In the internal affairs the early 1920s were characterized by the *sejmowładztwo* (the Seym dominance) resulting from the previously mentioned excessive power vested in the lower house of the legislature. The Cabinets were subject to the game played by the numerous parties which formed a short-lived coalitions. Piłsudski, while observing the helplessness and fickleness of rapidly changing coalition cabinets that were incapable of carrying out necessary reforms, was highly critical of the political scene. Whenever interviewed by press or asked for articulating his opinion, he blamed the politicians for corruption and incompetence and for preferring the interests of their parties to public good.

---

[1] Andrzej Chojnowski, *Piłsudski Józef*, [in:] *Wielka encyklopedia PWN*, Wydawnictwo Naukowe PWN, Warszawa 2004, vol. 21, p. 65.

[2] For more details on the problem see: Andrzej Leszek Szcześniak, *Historia 1918–1939*, Fundacja "Innowacja", Warszawa 1992, pp. 113–128.

The early twenties witnessed also the deterioration of Poland's position in the international scene since Germany tightened her links with the Soviet Russia (Rapallo pact of 1922 and the Berlin treaty of 1926). In addition, in the early 1926 the economic situation worsened. The unemployment grew. There was a lot of social unrest and some symptoms of the right-wing millieu contemplating the possibility of the coup. In these circumstances, the eyes of many politicians of various tint, including those of the left side, turned their eyes to Piłudski whom they considered a charismatic individual, capable of securing some stability and improvement.

And indeed, Piłsudski tried to meet the expectations. When there was formed the new governmental coalition of the Right and the Centre which, judging by its previous accomplishments, was little promising, Piłsudski and the troops faithful to him approached Warsaw. The armed demonstration itself proved however insufficient. The President refused to reorganize the Cabinet. There followed a few day's fighting which resulted in the President and the Prime Minister resigning their posts. The path to changes was open.

After the coup Piłsudski and his millieu of *Piłsudski-ties* were responsible for forming the authoritarian system of governing the country in which the emphasis was laid on the executive branch. The system that was thus introduced was referred to as the *Sanacja*, which smuggled the idea of moral cleansing of political life. Piłsudski himself emphasized his neutrality and avoided being identified with any specific party.

The constitutional change was carried out soon through the so called August Constitutional Amendment of 1926. According to it the President of the Republic had an effective, and not only the illusionary, chance to dissolve the parliament in certain circumstances. Also his competence to issue decrees and ordinancies grew while the Seym's right to adopt vote-of-no confidence vis-à-vis the government was a little diminished. Later, by 1935, the constitutional changes promoted by the *Piłsudski-ties* culminated in the adoption of the new Constitution which introduced certain devices of presidential system.

In order to consolidate their power the *Sanacja* millieu created the Non-Partisan Block of Cooperation with Government (BBWR). The representatives of various political groupings, varying from socialists to conservatists, were attracted by this government--sponsored party.

The first years that followed the May Coup were characterized by stabilization and relative prosperity due to the European temporary economic boom. At the same time however there began to grow certain friction between the parliamentarians and the *Sanacja* regime which frequently resorted to the use of the devices of amended constitutional law or to specific interpretation of constitutional clauses in order to bridle the criticism that might arise in the houses of the legislature. Many politicians began to believe that the accomplishments of the *Sanacja* fell short of the expectations. Piłsudski, in his turn, not infrequently expressed in public his scepticism toward the Seym deputies. On these occasions he sometimes used the abusive language.

The end of the 1920s witnessed the merger of the parties opposing the *Sanacja* into so called Centre-Left (*Centrolew*).[3] The latter began to blame the *Sanacja* for departing from the democratic standards. The criticism generated by the *Centrolew* began to reach the fora other than the floor of the parliament. The Congress that *Centrolew* organized in

---

[3] Witold Pronobis, *Polska i świat w XX wieku*. Editions Spotkania, Warszawa 1991, pp. 138–140.

June 1930 seemed – from the perspective of the *Sanacja* – to be particularly provocative. It went as far as demanding the taking of revolutionary steps against the regime and suggested the overthrowing of the President and the use of beyond-parliamentary measures in the fight against the post-May regime. In addition, the Congress called on the population to refrain from paying taxes and appealed to other states to refrain from granting any loans to Poland so long as the latter was the *Sanacja*-governed country.

In such atmosphere of social tension, in August 1930, the President dissolved the parliament. New elections were planned to be held in November. In early autumn the *Centrolew* launched a campaign of mass demonstrations in larger cities. That involved a threat of outbreak of a serious social unrest. While discussing with his millieu the possible developments Piłsudski said:

> ...the blood would be shed... Whose?... Certainly not that of the gentelmen who are the leaders! They would lick their lips because the blood thus spilled would be the grist to their mill.... No!... We must get even with the instigators themselves and not with the crowd whom they encourage to demonstrate in the streets against the police and the army.[4]

Encouraged by Piłsudski, the government decided to react radically. The leaders of the *Centrolew* were arrested. Many of them, were released later but some were brought to penal liability, tried in so called *Brzeski* trial and condemned to imprisonments that varied from 1,5 to 3 years. They were also offered the possibility of emigrating instead of serving their sentences.

Although the program of moral improvement of political life was generally accepted by the Poles, the detention of the opposition leaders and the information about sometimes brutal treatment that they experienced while detained, aroused a lot of social criticism.

In the 1930s the *Sanacja* was also blamed for organizing a camp of isolation in Bereza Kartuska where at average several hundred prisoners were kept. Most of the inmates were the radical activists of the ethnic minorities involved in terroristic actions. They were notoriously supported from the centres hostile to Poland and located abroad (Nazi Germany, Austria, Soviet Russia, but also Czechoslovakia or Lithuania). In some cases they were imprisoned on the basis of administrative decisions only without being subjected to regular trial. Their involvement in terrorism aroused no doubt but the regular trial might lead to the revealing of the information source which derived from the intelligence operations. From time to time the public opinion was moved by the news about unfair treatment of inmates in Bereza. The protests arising from that induced the government to react and bring those accused of the abuses to liability. Anyhow the rigour detectable in the Bereza Kartuska camp can by no means be compared with the dreadful conditions of the Nazi- or Soviet-organized labour camps.

The social unrest observable in Poland in the early 1930s was also generated by the world economic crisis ("the Great Slump"). In Poland the latter led first to the impoverishment of the rural population. The fall in the consumption consequently struck the industrial production. The investments came to a standstill. The unemployment grew.

---

[4] Władysław Pobóg-Malinowski, *Najnowsza historia polityczna Polski (1914–1939)*, Wydawnictwo Platan, Kraków 2004, vol. 2, pp. 715. The abridgements in the cited fragment were introduced after Szcześniak, *Historia*, p. 119.

In Poland the climax of the crisis fell upon 1932. The real improvement came as late as 1935. Only then Poland was able to launch a larger program of industrial development by forming at the confluence of the Vistula and the San rivers so called Central Industrial District (COP). Its forming was characterized by particular dynamism. Despite this effort Poland could not match the military production of Germany and Soviet Russia whose military industry much earlier worked at full speed.[5]

In the Communist historiography there was a tendency toward depicting Poland ruled by the *Sanacja* regime as the creation close to the fascist State. Such opinion swerves from the truth. The *Sanacja* regime was doubtless authoritarian but in fact it never fundamentally departed from the basic democratic standards. The censorship operated at a limited scale. Each day in Warsaw the daily *Kurier Warszawski* published by the National Democrats who opposed Piłsudski came out alongside with the *Piłsudski-ties Kurier Poranny*.[6] Although sometimes limited in their activities, the parties of the opposition could function and articulate their opinion. Only the parties of the extreme Left or the extreme Right might face restrictions. This referred in particular to the Communist Party of Poland (KPP) which used to challenge the independent status of the Republic and functioned as the Soviet-sponsored agency, or to the National Radical Camp (ONR) which promoted nationalistic and anti-semitic slogans and consequently was dissolved in the early 1930s.

It is interesting to note that the KPP, which was delegalized by the Polish authorities, was fully liquidated by the Comintern in 1938 on the basis of its alleged cooperation with the Polish intelligence. Its leaders were invited to Moscow and executed. Paradoxically only those of them survived who, by that time, served their sentences in Polish prisons.

In social life a lot of pluralism was observable in the *Sanacja* era. The youth could organize themselves along a lot of lines which involved scouting and groupings of various shade: nationalistic, religious, sports etc.[7] The same was true about the employees who could freely organize themselves in variety of trade unions.

In some areas the *Sanacja* was little successful. It could be blamed for small effects in seeking remedies that might prevent the impoverishment of the Polish society during the crisis of the early 1930s. Nor did the *Sanacja* politicians show sufficient understanding toward the national aspirations of the minorities. This referred particularly to the Ukrainians whose radicals, while supported from abroad, resorted to terrorism. In reprisal for that the police and the army reacted by pacification actions against the settlements suspected of collaboration with the terrorist groupings. On that occasion also a certain number of Ukrainian schools and other institutions were closed. Such policy only impeded the chance for reconciliation.

Among the positive aspects of the *Sanacja* era one may include the strengthening of the effectiveness of the executive power and consequently the strengthening of the State. This was badly needed in the face of the dangers arising from the growing hostility of Germany (which from 1933 was the Nazi Germany) and the Soviet Russia.

---

[5] Pronobis, *Polska*, p. 142, 171ff.

[6] Norman Davies, *God's Playground, A History of Poland*, Oxford University Press, Oxford 2005, vol. II, p. 317–318.

[7] Szczcśniak, *Historia*, pp. 113–128.

Józef Piłsudski, the founder of the *Sanacja*, died in 1935. Soon before his death the already mentioned April Constitution was adopted. It promoted the centralization of the power of the State, particularly its executive branch.

In this brief outline of Piłsudski's silhouette some remarks on his concept referring to the arrangement of Poland's foreign policy are indispensable. After World War I he thought about forming a barrier against expanding Russia by promoting the creation of a series of democratic states that would stretch from Finland to the area close to the Caucasus, and be bound by some alliance with Poland. This contradicted the plans of the Bolsheviks who tried to spread the flame of the red revolt throughout the entire Europe. As a result the Polish-Bolshevik war broke out in 1919–1920. During this war Piłsudski demonstrated his military talent. He considerably contributed – through his risky but successful tactical maneuvers – to the defeat of the large Red Army at the battle of Warsaw in summer 1920.[8] This victorious battle is often referred to as the "miracle at the Vistula" since it fell upon the Feast of Assumption of Our Lady, Queen of Poland. The battle rescued the rest of Europe from being invaded by the Red Army. Such invasion was what was in the Lenin's and Trotsky's contemplation by that time. In his memoires, Tukhachevsky, who commanded the campaign against Poland, wrote:

> There is the least doubt that, if we were victorious at the Vistula, the revolution would spread its flame throughout the entire European land.[9]

In the years that followed, Piłsudski worked out the strategy of keeping equal distance vis-à-vis the two neighbour countries: Germany and Russia which permanently demonstrated their enmity toward Poland. Piłsudski maintained that although Poland could sign with them the non-agression pacts nevertheless she should never enter with any of the two into any mutual assistance pact.

When Piłsudski died (1935), the foreign policy pattern that he established was followed by his successors in the ship of State. As a result Poland never became the satellite of either Germany or Russia. Instead, just before the outbreak of World War II, she managed to persuade Great Brittain and France to sign mutual assistance pacts with her.

Out of the rich range of Piłsudski's accomplishments the present paper, in its further fragment, will focuse on more detailed discussion of his achievements of the years 1914–1918, designed to restore Poland's statehood. In that context there will be presented his relationships, based on both compromise and conflict, first with the Austro-Hungarian, and – when the war progressed – also with the German authorities.

2. *Piłsudski's Scenario of Regaining Independence. Its Early Development*

The years preceding the outbreak of World War I witnessed a considerable animation among the Poles. The point was that the powers which at one time partitioned Poland found themselves in hostile camps. Austro-Hungary and Germany (with Prussia as its part)

---

[8] Chojnowski, *Piłsudski*, p. 65.

[9] Tukhachevsky is quoted by Pronobis, *Polska*, p. 72.

made up the core of Central Powers while Russia entered into an alliance with France and Great Brittain forming so called *Entente Cordiale*.

As has already been said, in the years preceding the outbreak of war Piłsudski concentrated his activities in Austrian Poland. This was the part of Poland where Poles enjoyed relatively large proportion of freedom. Therefore Piłsudski selected this area to form in it the nucleus of Polish military force which, he believed, would be badly needed in the chaos that would inevitably follow the disintegration of the three partitioning empires. That such disintegration was unavoidable was, in his opinion, beyond all doubts. It was as early as January 1914 that Piłsudski delivered a lecture at the Geographic Institute of Paris. On the basis of this lecture Victor M. Chernov, an outstanding leader of the Russian Social Revolutionary Party, produced a report which emphasized the major points of Piłsudski's concluding remarks. Wrote he:

> Piłsudski clearly prophesied an Austro-Russian war for the Balkans in the near future. He had no doubts that behind Austria will stand – and even now secretly stands – Germany. He further expressed conviction that France would not be allowed to remain a passive spectator of the conflict: the day when Germany will openly side with Austria will be the eve of the day when France, by virtue of her alliance, will intervene on the side of Russia. Finally, Great Britain, he thought, could not afford to leave France to her fate. Should the united forces of France and England be not sufficient they will, sooner or later, drag America into the war on their side. Analyzing further the military potential of all these countries Piłsudski clearly stated the problem: how would the war develop, with whose victory would it end? His answer was: Russia was bound to be beaten by Austria and Germany, and they in turn would be defeated by the Anglo-French (or Anglo-American-French) coalition.[10]

No wonder that for such a far-sighted individual like Piłsudski the forming of the foundations of the Polish army was a challenging task. It was as early as 1908 that in Austrian Poland, in Galicia, there came to being the Organization of Active Struggle (*Związek Walki Czynnej*) with J. Piłsudski, K. Sosnkowski and M. Kukiel at its head. The organization was soon responsible for supervising the legally formed paramilitary organisations such as the Rifle Association (*Związek Strzelecki*) in Lvov and the Rifle Society (*Towarzystwo Strzeleckie*) in Cracow.[11] It was in these organizations that Polish patriotic youth received their first military training.

Piłsudski belonged to the millieu of so called "activists". He tried to encourage the Poles to engage themselves in direct fight for Poland's independence.[12] In their first impulse they should, he thought, side Austria in her fight against Russia. But their commitment to the cause of Austria should not be total. In due time the restoring of independent Poland would become for them the major goal to achieve.

The World War I broke out in summer 1914 upon the assassination in Sarajevo of Archduke Ferdinand, successor to the Austro-Hungarian throne. Before any larger hostilities took place between the belligerent states there began to develop the Piłsudski's project designed to lead the Poles to independence. Piłsudski believed that his *Rifles*,

---

[10] Quoted after Kamil Dziewanowski, *Poland in the 20th Century*, Columbia Univ. Press, New York, 1977, pp. 65–66.

[11] Pronobis, *Polska*, pp. 32–33.

[12] Norman Davies, *Heart of Europe. A Short History of Poland*, Clarendon Press, Oxford 1984, p. 111.

upon crossing the boarder dividing Austria from Russia-controlled Congress Poland, might organize sabotage actions on the territory of enemy and even trigger off the rising against the Russians. He himself believed that his reconnaissance group, when enlarged by the volunteers from the Russian partition, would make up the army composed of the individuals who were not the subjects of the Austrian Emperor. That would secure the relative independence of the force that he tended to create and that might be the nucleus of the army of the future independent state.

And indeed the Austrians allowed for Piłsudski's mobilization of his men who, as the first regular Company of Rifles, progressed as far as Kielce in the Congress Poland and tried to recruit volunteers into their ranks. The entire action ended however in failure. The Austrians did not provide it with sufficient support. Besides, in Congress Poland the society was unprepared to national awakening. The last insurrection against Russians was that of 1863. It was brutally suppressed. After its failure the Poles focused on so called *organic work* whose program – instead of military action – promoted the attaining of peaceful goals: decrease in poverty, elimination of illiteracy, development of culture etc.

Paradoxically one may speculate that if the rising in the Congress Poland really broke out it would inevitably engage Russian forces which therefore would not sufficiently resist the pressure of German troops advancing from East Prussia. If that happened, Germany, after a shortly obtained victory in the East, might consequently redeploy some part of their army to the West. This, in its turn, might prevent the French armies from being successful in staying the course of German advances at the Marne in September 1914.[13] If worst came to worst the Germans might then carry out the Schlieffen's plan of crushing the French in six weeks' campaign and consequently avoid the war on two fronts. On a long run that would badly affect also Polish perspectives. Further developments showed that first the defeat of Russia at hand of Central Powers and then a mortal blow dealt on them by Western Allies opened the path leading to *Polonia Restituta*.

When Piłsudski's plan in the Congress Poland ended in failure, the disappointed Austrians demanded his resignation and incorporation of his soldiers into the Austrian army. Fortunately however a new scenario began to develop. The point was that exactly at that time the Polish deputies to the Vienna parliament applied to the Austrian Emperor for accepting the idea of forming the Polish legions under the auspices of Austria. The Emperor gave his consent to this plan. The Austrians would provide the legionaries with the uniforms and weapons. The soldiers, in their turn, would have to swear a regular oath of loyalty to the Emperor and remain under a general command of the Austrian generals. Also at that time, in Galicia, in Cracow, there was formed the Supreme National Committee (*Naczelny Komitet Narodowy*) which aspired at having a political supervision over the legions. The members of the committee recruited themselves from the conservatists, socialists, nationalists and peasant representatives. They counted on the enlargement of the Austrian part of Poland by the territories that previously made up the Russian partition. That would facilitate the transformation of the Habsburg monarchy into a trialist state which would put on the same footing not only Austria and Hungary but also Poland. The Austrian Emperor, although originally friendly-disposed toward

---

[13] Dziewanowski, *Poland*, p. 67.

that concept, surrended later to the Hungarian and German pressure, which contested this project.[14]

Although that scenario fell short of Piłsudski's expectations he accepted the accomplished facts and consented to being the commander of the first regiment of legions. This regiment soon turned into the legendary First Brigade. Like the rest of the legions thus also its First Brigade successfully engaged themselves in resisting the Russian offensive in 1914 and 1915. Polish soldiers distinguished themselves in a series of battles such as those of Konary, Jastków, Łowczówek etc. Their cavalry became famous for its desperate but successful uhlan charge at Rokitna.

In late autumn 1916 the Russians under the command of Brusilov managed, with an enormous effort, to hit the Austrians a hard blow and break their lines in the eastern front. Polish legions were fully involved in heavy fight against the Russian pressure. The success of the Russians was however of only short-lived effect. Yet what the Russians brought into effect was the total exhaustion of the Austrian army. Though Brusilov's campaign was stopped, the Austrians, from that time on, played little role in the war, thereby yielding precedence to Germany. The Germans, in their turn, while seizing the vast territories in the east, replaced Russians, and consequently became, together with Austrians, the new occupiers of what at one time was the Polish-Lithuanian Commonwealth. The area of the previous Congress Kingdom was divided into a German occupation zone with the centre in Warsaw, where governor Hans von Beseler had his seat, and the Austrian zone which had its centre in Lublin. The area extending eastwards beyond the Bug was organized into Oberkommando-Ost and had its major seat in Wilna.

It was in the area, previously controlled by the Russians that, even before it was seized by the Central powers, Piłsudski tried to consolidate the activities of the previously mentioned and clandestinely active Polish Military Organization (POW). In its ranks there could be found militarily trained men who, according to Piłsudski's plans, were assigned the task of future fight for fully independent Poland. In the meantime the organization was engaged in intelligence operations and diversion at the rear of Russian army. By 1916 the conspiratorial organization amounted to about 13.000 soldiers in 17 clandestine districts. The individuals from various ranks of society could be found among the POW members, 50% being peasants, 15% workers, the rest representing intelligentsia, burghers and landowners.

What deserves some emphasis are also the activities of the Polish emigration in the West. It was as early as 1914, and throughout 1915 that a lot of Polish organizations abroad, in the USA, Switzerland or England, engaged themselves in soliciting Poland's independence and rendering assistance to the Polish population that experienced a lot of suffering on the territories affected by the war hostilities.[15]

---

[14] Andrzej Albert, *Najnowsza historia Polski 1914–1993*, Wydawnictwo Puls, Londyn 1994, p. 29ff.

[15] Albert, *Najnowsza historia*, pp. 30–31.

3. *Programs other than those of Piłsudski*

Apart from the line followed by Polish patriots in the Austrian partition, there was also another one promoted by those who, particularly in the Congress Kingdom but also in other partition zones, were affected by Roman Dmowski's political concepts. In the years preceding the war, Dmowski, the leader of Polish National Party (*Polskie Stronnictwo Narodowe*), was an outstanding politician, particularly active in the circle of Polish deputies to Russian Duma, which was the parliament that was allowed to function in the empire of the Tsar by virtue of the 1906 Russian Constitution. This Constitution allowed for forming certain devices of constitutional monarchy although in fact it served as a screen behind which autocracy could survive. Dmowski, observing the discrimination of the Poles in Prussia, which from 1870s was a part of the second German Reich, believed that siding Russia was the best option to the Poles. He hoped that Russia's alliance with France would incite the deepening of Russian democracy. Thus, upon the end of the war, the Poles – he believed – might count on being granted a considerable autonomy under the septre of the Tsar.[16] Dmowski and the supporters of his concept were referred to as the *passivists* in which they differed from those who advocated the Piłsudski's plans and who were called the *activists*.

What was the grist to Dmowski's mill was the fact that in August 1914 Grand Duke Nicholas, commander of the Eastern front, issued a proclamation in which one might read of "Poland reborn" out of the territories of the three partitions, which, after the defeat of Austrian and German armies, would be united under the septre of the Tsar. The allusions to freedom of faith, language and self-rule were made. However the promise contained in the proclamation remained a dead letter since Russians were soon driven away from the area inhabited by the Poles.

Apart from Piłsudski's and Dmowski's programs there was also detectable the line represented by the left of the communist tint. Its supporters were grouped in the party called Social Democracy of the Polish Kingdom and Lithuania (SDKPiL). The Communists were far from promoting any tendencies aimed at forming independent Poland. They gave priority to the Europe-wide Communist revolt.

4. *The Central Powers' Attitude toward the Polish Question. The Manifesto of 6 November 1916*

In fact the war developments followed the line, that Piłsudski foresaw as early as 1914. The Russians were practically defeated in the east. While withdrawing from the Congress Kingdom, they evacuated from it both a lot of industrial property as well a considerable number of the population.[17]

---

[16] Norman Davies, *God's Playground. A History of Poland*, Oxford University Press 2005, vol. II, pp. 39–40, 281. Thus Dmowski was the advocate of the pro-Russian orientation, on that see more details in: Albert, *Najnowsza historia*, p. 29ff.

[17] Albert, *Najnowsza historia*, p. 29.

With the defeat of the Russians, the role of the legions as supporters of the cause of Central Powers (Germany, Austria) began to lose sense from the perspective of the Polish reason of state. If the legions continued playing their previous role they might only impede the efforts of the allied in the West in their campaign against Germany. This did not lie in the interest of the Poles who thought about the restoration of their statehood.

Despite driving the Russians away from the Congress Kingdom the Central Powers were silent about the Polish question. They did not put forth any project that would be satisfactory to the Poles.[18] Piłsudski therefore suspended the recruitment of new men to the legions and, instead, began to develop the conspiratorial POW organization which, engaged in intelligence operations, was charged with the mission of preparing armed fight for independence.

What additionally increased Piłsudski's reserve toward the cooperation with Central Powers was the strict subjection of the legions to the Austrian command. Stiff attitude of Central Powers in this respect, despite sacrifices made by the Poles, disappointed Piłsudski. Another source of his disappointment was too loyal pro-Austrian stance adopted by the Supreme National Committee which – as has already been said – functioned in Galicia since mid-1914 and aspired at exercising political authority over the legions. In these circumstances Piłsudski was determined to resign his position in the legionary army. In autumn 1916 he applied to the Austrians for being dismissed. His request was accepted.

At the same time the council of legionary colonels drew up a memorial in which they demanded that the legions be turned into a separate and independent army. And indeed Emperor Francis Joseph thought about forming the Polish auxiliary Corps amounting to two divisions. That however would require also the consent of Germany which had ever larger influence on the decisions taken by the Central Power's coalition.[19]

At the end of 1916 there seemed however to emerge another project that the Poles could not ignore. The needs of long and exhaustive war which Germany and Austria had to wage on the two fronts rendered them prepared for making new concessions to the Poles. And indeed on 6 November 1916 Hans Beseler, German Governor of Warsaw, in cooperation with the Austrian Governor of Lublin, declared, in the name of the Austrian and German Emperors, the willingness of the latter to form, within the area conquered by them, the Kingdom of Poland with hereditary monarch, constitutional system and its own army.[20] The scope of sovereignty and the boundries of the new Kingdom were left non-specified. The declaration was issued in the form of the Manifesto. It was easy to guess that in fact the Austrian and German authorities tended toward encouraging the Polish males who were neither citizens of Austria nor of Germany and who therefore were not subject to general conscription, to enter the ranks of occupying armies.

Since the Russian emperor did not want to lag behind the rulers of Austria and Germany he also tried to win the sympathy of the Poles on the area which in fact he no longer controlled. In the order that he issued at the end of 1916 he made an allusion to the assistance that Russia could render to the Poles in re-uniting their motherland. He argued that one of the goals of the war was

---

[18] *Ibidem*, p. 30.

[19] *Ibidem*.

[20] Pronobis, *Polska*, pp. 34–35.

the forming of the independent Polish state composed of all the territories in which the Poles dominate.[21]

A few months later Russia was swept by revolutionary upheaval and the tsarism was overthrown.

While realistically assessing the promise made in their Manifestos by the Austrian and German Emperors one would have to find that the new Kingdom of Poland would be territorially limited. Neither Austria nor Germany would easily resign from Silesia, Pomerania, parts of Galicia etc. Further developments showed that also the forming of an independent Polish government would inevitably face considerable impediments.

Nevertheless Piłsudski, while drawing on the discussed declaration tried to exploit this new chance for the implementation of his program aimed at independent Poland. There was therefore formed – in the Piłsudski's millieu – the Central National Committee. It accepted the goals promoted by the two Emperors' Manifesto but demanded that the Polish autonomous government be created since only such government would be the authorized dispenser of the Polish blood.[22]

In December 1916 the occupiers consented to the forming on territory of the late Congress Kingdom of the provisional Council of State (later replaced by the Regency Council). The members of this body were nominated by the German authorities. Piłsudski also became the member of the Council. He was responsible for its military department. He however was soon disappointed with the Council's limited competence and consequently its small prestige among the Poles.[23]

In early July 1917, on occasion of his meeting with the group of senior legionary officers, Piłsudski frankly admitted that he tended toward provoking a conflict with the Austrian and German military authorities. What he planned was the refusal of swearing an oath of loyalty to the Emperor by those legionaries who were not the citizens of Austro-Hungary. Piłsudski argued that in view of the fall of tsarism in Russia the idea of following the joint path by the Poles and Germans had come to an end. Said he:

> At present our interests and those of the Germans contradict one another. It is the defeating of the allied that lies in the interest of the Germans while it is in our interest that the Germans be defeated by the allied.[24]

At a certain moment the German authorities began to consider transformation of the legions into some kind of the Polish Verhrmacht. In July 1917 an offer was also made to transfer the Piłsudski's allegiance from Austria to Germany. Piłsudski's negative answer to that proposal was firm, which was detectable in his conversation with Hans Beseler, Governor of Warsaw, in July 1917. Beseler tried to tempt Piłsudski with the mirage of power, fame and money. The course of the conversation between the two was as follows:

---

[21] Cited after Pronobis, *Polska*, p. 33.

[22] *Ibidem*, p. 32; see also Pronobis, *Polska*, p. 35.

[23] Pronobis, *Polska*, p. 35.

[24] *Ibidem*.

Piłsudski: Your Excellency, do you imagine for one moment that you will win the nation's confidence by hanging Polish insignia on each of the fingers of the hand which is throttling Poland? The Poles know the Prussian stranglehold for what it is.
von Beseler: Herr von Piłsudski, you know that in these stirring times Poland needs a leader of vision, and you are the only one whom i have been able to find. If you go along with us, we will give you everything – power, fame, money...
Piłsudski: Your Excellency, does not understand me, and does not wish to understand. If I were to go along with you, Germany would gain one man, whilst I would lose a nation.[25]

5. International Dimension of the Polish Question

In the meantime Polish question began to appear in the pronouncements of rulers and statesman of the time. Apart from the already mentioned Manifesto of the German and Austro-Hungarian Emperors and the declaration of Nicolaus II (Dec. 1916), also US President Woodrow Wilson, in his Message to Senate of January 1917, suggested the restoring of the united and independent Poland in the post war-organized Europe. The activities of the American Poles, including those of famous Polish composer Ignacy Paderewski, were formative of his position. Soon after, in April 1917 the United States themselves entered into the war on the side of *Entente*.

With the fall of tsarism in Russia, which was swept by the revolutionary forces, the hopes of the Poles had a larger chance to come true. In March 1917 the Petrograd Council of the Delegates of Workers and Soldiers acknowledged the rights of the Poles to self-determination. This encouraged the Russian Provisional Government to produce a similar declaration.[26] This, in its turn, gave rise to a remarkable animation of the Poles who in large number found themselves in Russia of the time including half million of those who served in the Russian army, a remarkable number detectable among the Austrian and German prisoners of war and a great number of civilians.[27] As a result there were formed in Russia various Polish military troops. Unfortunately also in their ranks there spread the revolutionary ferment that was typical of the Russian army. Particularly the Communists were against the forming of the Polish national army since they staked their hopes in the Europe-wide revolution that they tried to incite.

The constitutional transformation in Russia allowed the Western Powers (Great Britain, France) to adopt a positive attitude toward the Polish question. Previously they had their hands tied up by the need to respect the opinion of the Tsar since he was the ally of their coalition. In the new circumstances this was not necessary. No wonder that quite soon also President of France Raymond Poincaré signed the decree that allowed for the forming of the Polish autonomous army in France, composed mostly of the volunteers derived from the pre-war emigrants but recruited also from the Poles arriving from the United States, Canada and Brazil.[28]

---

[25] The conversation is cited by Norman Davies, *God's Playground*, pp. 284–285.

[26] Albert, *Najnowsza historia*, p. 33; see also Norman Davies, *God's Playground*, vol. II, p. 285.

[27] Albert, *Najnowsza historia*, p. 34.

[28] *Ibidem*, p. 35.

Next year, in January 1918, US President Woodrow Wilson in one of his Fourteen Points put forth a demand that "a united, independent, and autonomous Poland with free unstriced access to the sea", be restored.[29]

6. Piłsudski's Volta

The developments of 1917 showed that the image of the united and independent Poland was ever more seriously treated by the leading personalities of international scene. In these circumstances Piłsudski resigned from his position in the Provisional Council of State and, as has already been said earlier, he laid the emphasis on invigorating the secret Polish Military Organization. When the German authorities refused his offer of exploiting this organization as the structure formative of the Polish Military Force, Piłsudski was fully determined to provoke a conflict with the Germans and consequently to refuse to militarily cooperate with them. And indeed, by July 1917, he refused to swear an oath of loyalty to the provisional Polish authorities that were subject to Germany and Austro-Hungary. Most of the soldiers of the Legions followed his pattern, thereby being dismissed and interned. The soldiers who were of Austro-Hungarian citizenship were incorporated into the Austrian army.[30] Polish commanders, including Piłsudski, were arrested, Piłsudski himself being imprisoned in the fortress of Magdeburg.[31]

7. Polish Representatives in the West

In the context of these developments worthy of note is also the evolution of Dmowski's line which at one time seemed to lead to at least some autonomy of the territories inhabited by the Poles. As has already been mentioned Dmowski promoted the pro-Russian choice. He believed that the Poles, while supporting Russia in the Great War, might count on arriving at large concessions as granted to them by the Romanoff rulers of this country. However with the defeats of Russia in 1915, and particularly with the seizure by the Central Powers of the area of Congress Poland and their further progress to the East, Dmowski was deprived of the basis on which his arguments for siding Russia could develop. Russia as guarantor of autonomous Poland sounded little realistic and reliable. Of no help was the already mentioned declaration of Tsar Nicholaus II produced at the end of 1916 in which the ruler of Russia pronounced that one of the goals of the war waged by Russia was "the restoring of free Poland composed of the three hitherto separated parts".[32]

In fact already earlier, by the end of 1915, Dmowski left Russia for the West, spent some time in London and Lousanna (in Switzerland) to be later active in Paris during the Versailles Conference. He made a lot of efforts to establish the position of his KNP (Polish National Committee) as the exclusive representative of the future Polish gover-

---

[29] Norman Davies, *God's Playground*, vol. II, p. 286.

[30] Pronobis, *Polska*, p. 35.

[31] *Ibidem.*

[32] Quoted after Albert, *Najnowsza historia*, p. 33.

nment.[33] It was him who submitted to the representatives of *Entente* the memorial that demanded the forming of independent Poland. In this memorial he tried to outline the frontiers of the State that was being restored.

8. *Polonia Restituta*

In the era directly preceding the end of the Great War there functioned in the previous Congress Kingdom – still formally occupied by the Central Powers – the Regency Council which replaced the previous Council of State. Although in the final stage of its activities the Regency Council was trying to secure for itself a larger degree of independence vis-à-vis the declining authority of the Austrian and German occupiers, it was rather incapable of winning the support of various political groupings which sprang up among the patriotically-disposed Poles. The Council was considered to be too conservative and too conciliatory. What was particularly disappointing to the Poles was the treaty of Brest-Litovsk of March 1918 – signed by Germany with Soviet Russia. The Poles had no share in negotiating it while the treaty proved to be particularly detrimental to the Polish territorial interests.

In view of the rapid developments on the European scene, and particularly the disintegration of the Central Powers that were convulsed by the internal, often left-oriented disorders, the appearance in Warsaw – by November 1918 – of Józef Piłsudski, released from the Magdeburg prison, provided a chance of consolidating around him a large spectre of adherents. Among them there were those who remembered his determination in supporting the cause of independent Poland as well as those who did not forget his earlier predisposition to socialistic values. Unlike the Communists who surrendered to internationalistic slogans and counted on Europe-wide red revolt, thereby rejecting the concept of *Polonia Restituta*, the moderate socialists who supported Piłsudski advocated the re-birth of their motherland. In it they planned to introduce deep social reforms through the instruments of parliamentary democracy. They rejected the anarchist leanings of Bolsheviks.

Upon the arrival of Piłsudski the Regency Council entrusted full power to him. He was proclaimed Chief of the State and charged with the mission of forming the temporary government. As a result he became the Head of the State the boundaries of which were not yet fixed and whose organizational structure was *in statu nascendi*. The nation-wide character of this government was soon recognized by the regional committees which in a series of places began to form the nuclei of the restored statehood (Poznań, Teschen, Lvov, Lublin).

The spontaneous developments in Poland thwarted Dmowski's and his millieu's designs that were worked out in Paris. The Paris group had to face the accomplished facts which amounted to the emergence of the domestic government in Warsaw. On the other hand it was Dmowski and his group of National Democrats who monopolized the foreign policy of the reemerging State and it was them who were regarded by the European Powers as the only representation of Poland. Some compromise, between those active at home and those active abroad had to be achieved. And indeed it was. The symbol of the

---

[33] Norman Davies, *God's Playground*, vol. II, p. 285.

compromise was Ignacy Paderewski, a famous composer and pianist, connected with the Paris group which was headed by Dmowski. It was Paderewski whom, in early 1919, Piłsudski charged with the mission of forming the coalition government composed of the representatives of a large range of groupings that varied from socialistic politicians to those of the National Democratic Right. Shortly after this, the first elections to the Legislative Seym were proclaimed. Poland began to function on its own.

Józef Piłsudski's Attitude toward the Cause of Austria and Germany in World War I

Summary

The paper discusses the share of Józef Piłsudski, a charismatic leader of the Poles, in the restoring of the Polish statehood during World War I. What was emphasized was the Piłsudski's far-sightedness. In a series of lectures that he delivered in Paris before the outbreak of the war, he with a surprising precision foresaw the war developments and the disintegration of the three empires that at one time partitioned Poland. This, in his opinion, would produce a space within which Poland's statehood might be restored. Piłsudski therefore made a large effort to form – during the war – the Polish army which at first was expected to side one of the empires involved in the war. For that purpose Piłsudski selected the Habsburg monarchy as the most liberal partitioner of the Polish land. Later, when in the course of the war the Polish question began to assume international dimension, he persisted in securing ever more independent status for his army. He tried to loosen its tie with the Central Powers. This inevitably led to his clash with their authorities. Piłsudski's committment to the concept of *Polonia Restituta* and the risky game that he played with both the German and Austrian authorities won the confidence of the Poles to him. After the war his impact on the developments in Poland was significant. He is particularly remembered for his share in defeating the Bolshevik army that invaded Poland on 1920. The strategy that Piłsudski applied on that occasion led to the dramatic but victorious battle at the Vistula in summer this year. Poland's victory prevented Western Europe from being flooded by the Red Army.

ANDRZEJ DZIADZIO

The Role Played by the Constitutional Tribunal in Preserving the Liberal Nature of the Habsburg Monarchy at the Turn of the 19th Century

It was on the basis of the constitutional laws of 21 December 1867 that were referred to as the December Constitution that the Austrian monarchy became the first European *Rechtsstaat*. Upon the *Ausgleich* with the Hungarians the Austrian Constitution reflected all these significant components of the German concept of *Rechtsstaat* that could not be brought into effect at the time of the Springtime of Nations 1848–1849. Among them there were the priority as given to the Constitution, separation of powers, subjecting the State apparatus to law, independent courts and independent judges as well as the catalogue of civil rights and liberties.[1] The constitutional law on the universal civil rights of 1867 contained the most developed system of the rights of an individual in Europe of the time. It is until now that the basic rights (Grundrechte) contained in this law specify the constitutional scope of civil rights in Austria.

What was however the major guarantor of securing the constitutional order were the three tribunals of public law: the Constitutional Tribunal (*Reichsgericht*), the Administrative Tribunal (*Verwaltungsgerichtshof*), and the Tribunal of State (*Staatsgerichtshof*). Although the Constitutional Tribunal which functioned from 1869 was not competent to check whether the laws were consistent with the Constitution, nevertheless it safeguarded the Constitution since it examined the complaints filed by the citizens against the State agencies' infringements of the Constitution-guaranteed basic rights.

The Administrative Tribunal, which came to being in 1876, examined, in its turn, the complaints against these administrative decisions which infringed the law. Upon finding them illegal, the Tribunal quashed them. The Tribunal of State, in its turn, was the institution whose task was to try the ministers who infringed the Constitution and the laws. This Tribunal was a successful instrument (resembling the American Supreme Court which would try impeachment cases) which was designed to lay the foundations of the constitutional responsibility of the high-positioned public functionaries of the Rechtsstaat. In the 20th century this instrument was accepted inter alia in Poland.

---

[1] A. Dziadzio, *Koncepcja państwa prawa w XIX wieku – idea i rzeczywistość*, "Czasopismo Prawno-Historyczne", vol. LVII, 2005, z. 1, p. 186.

In Austria, on account of its constitutional function the most important guarantor of the liberal constitutional order was the Constitutional Tribunal. This Tribunal acquired a high-ranking position in the Austrian system of constitutional monarchy. This was among others due to the fact that those who were sitting in it were the most outstanding representatives of the world of learning that recruited themselves from all the significant centres (Vienna, Prague, Cracow, Lvov). It was Józef Unger (d. 1913), the most eminent civilist of the time,[2] who for 32 years was the president of the Constitutional Tribunal. The Constitutional Tribunal gained a high ranking reputation in the eyes of the Austrian public opinion also because while examining the ideological or political questions that were important from the point of view of the State authorities it proved capable of issuing the decisions in defiance of the State agencies' expectations. Thus, in 1886, it opposed the State agencies' attempts to introduce a ban on the establishing by the Old Catholics their own religious associations, the ban in question being motivated by the tendency to defend the Catholic character of the State.

The Austrian bureaucracy treated the decisions issued by the Constitutional Tribunal as a set of legal principles that took on character of precedents because the complaints that were filed with the Tribunal aimed at the obtaining by those who filed them of the binding interpretation of the sense of constitutional civil rights and liberties. This interpretation was arrived at through the considering of specific decisions of administrative agencies such as the prohibition of the activities of certain associations. Without any exaggeration one may say that the State apparatus treated the decisions of the Constitutional Tribunal as the *Twelve Tables* of the Austrian constitutional law. Despite the fact that the decisions of the Tribunal were only of declarative (moral) nature, in practice they were fully implemented by the administration.

The constitutional system introduced in 1867 by the December Constitution laid the foundations for many political and social tendencies among various groupings in Austria. In the course of time these groupings began to regard the liberal and multinational character of the State as an impediment to reach the purposes that they planned to achieve. What became particularly anticonstitutional was the nationalistic movement of Germans in Austria. Its social significance grew after Kazimierz Badeni's Cabinet introduced, by 1897, the linguistic equality in the area of the Czech Crown. The Germans considered themselves humilated by this regulation since the latter provided that all officials would have to have a good command of two languages. That meant that the Germans would have to necessarily learn Czech if they wanted to continue holding their official posts.

The German nationalistic movement in Austria was anti-Habsburg, anti-Slavic, anti-semitic and anti-Catholic. The nationalists put forth the slogan promoting their separation from Austria since they tended *irredenta Germanica, zu bilden* under the septre of the Hohenzollerns. They inspired the emergence of the social movement that was referred to as *Los von Rom*. The movement called on the Germans to leave the Catholic Church and join the Protestant denomination as "the national" German religion. This movement patronized also the initiative that was called *Freie Schule*. The objective of the latter was to liberate the school instruction from the influence of the Catholic religion.

---

[2] *Idem, Monarchia konstytucyjna w Austrii 1867–1914. Władza. Obywatel. Prawo*, Księgarnia Akademicka, Kraków 2002, p. 64.

In 1885 the program of the German nationalistic movement was supplemented by the "Aryan" paragraph which forbade the admittance to this party the individuals of Jewish extraction. Apart from the nationalistic movement there also came to being the German Radical Party which demanded the separation of the Church from the State, the secular school, and the fully secularized matrimonial law. The propaganda of nationalistic movement usually led to the abuse of freedom of speech and press. The State apparatus tried to suppress the xenophobia and racism and in making the efforts to do this was supported by the Constitutional Tribunal. The latter, as a rule, regarded as consistent with the Constitution the decisions of the authorities that prohibited the activities of the societies that promoted the racist programs.

Apart from the nationalistic tendencies, equally strong – in the declining years of the Austrian monarchy – was also the drift toward the secularization of the State. The fight for the secular nature of State and law was made by the circles of the Vienna liberal press linked with the lay Jewish millieu. Sometimes this fight put on the character of the crusade against the Catholic Church. Those who actively joined that fight were the Austrian Socialdemocrats. Also the groups of the Vienna modernism fought against the Catholic tradition. It was Sigismund Freud's psychoanalysis which became the "ideology" of modernism. At the turn of the 20th century the public life in Austria was almost tantamount to *bellum ominium contra omnes*.

The blow dealt upon the State and the Catholic Church caused that the two institutions yielded to the syndrom of the "besieged fortress". Because indeed they were attacked from various sides: by nationalism, libertinism, socialism and modernism. That led to the forming of a natural alliance between the State and the Church, the alliance being patronized by successor to the throne Archduke Francis Ferdinand who inter alia became the President of the Catholic Scholastic Association. The Court new elite sought the support of the Church which was the strongest public corporation that did not contest the Habsburg State. The already extreme old age of Emperor Francis Joseph I caused that the reins of the government tended to shift into the hands of the successor to the throne. The decided support secured by Francis Ferdinand to the Church institutions was a visible sign encouraging the authorities to undertake the activities that defended the Catholic character of the State.

The political hinterland of the discussed alliance was partly made up by the Christian-Social Party whose program resounded also with the nationalistic and anti-Semitic slogans but on the other hand demonstrated the pro-Habsburg attitude. In its ideology the slogan *Los von Rom,* was set against the concept *Los von Rom ist los von Österreich.* The fact that in these circumstances there followed no far-reaching clericalism of the Austrian State structures was due to the Constitutional Tribunal which, in its decisions, opposed the suppression of the freethinking societies. Before the Constitutional Tribunal the state authorities did not try to conceal their attitude. They demonstrated that they with all possible means tended toward delegalizing such societies.[3] The Constitutional Tribunal did not give its consent however to stigmatizing the lay societies with anti-State or anarchistic tendencies. It expressly let the State apparatus learn that the negative opinion

---

[3] *Idem, Ochrona praw i wolności obywatelskich w austriackiej monarchii konstytucyjnej (1867–1914),* "Czasopismo Prawno-Historyczne", vol. LIII, 2001, z. 1, p. 267.

on these societies could be authorized if made by the State as the exponent of the Catholic part of the society but not if made by the State as an organization that represented the interests of all citizens. Thus in its decisions the Tribunal defended the principles of the State as the entity that was liberal and that met the requirements of the *Rechtsstaat.*

At the decline of its existence the Austrian monarchy went through the days of permanent ideological and cultural war. The political situation of the Austrian monarchy of the time was paradoxical since the conservative State apparatus, together with the centrally-positioned Courts and Tribunals defended the legal order against the pressure of "civil society" which tried to fashion the state after its own mould. Some tended to have the State that would protect the rights of only one nation, the remaining part of the society being boiled down to the second category citizens. Others demanded the secular State in which the Catholic Church would be eliminated from public life.

The supreme Austrian Tribunals, and particularly the Constitutional Tribunal, may take the credit for the fact that, in spite of the pressure exerted on them by various social and political factors, they managed to preserve the liberal and constitutional order in Austria until 1914. The positive myth of Francis Joseph I's monarchy survived although in fact the monarchy was the scene of incessant national struggles. The latter eventually put down to its fall. The survival of the myth was due to the fact that despite numerous conflicts and disputes the Austrian monarchy remained until its last days the *Rechtsstaat* that defended the rights of its citizens irrespective of their national, denominational or political affiliation.

On the turn of the 20th century there was however observed a process of partial departure from the liberal assumptions of the December Constitution of 1867. Two selected examples of the decisions issued by the Administrative Tribunal and the Constitutional Tribunal in the area of freedom of religion and conscience may be illustrative of that. The first case referred to the 1870 statute-guaranteed possibility of adopting by the Austrian citizen the non-denominational status. This status allowed for contracting before the State officer the secular marriage and consequently made the divorce available. The second case referred to the statutory principle accepted in those days and pronouncing that the contributions and fees for the benefit of Churches and religious unions might be collected exclusively from the individuals who belonged to these organizations.

On the basis of provisions on the non-denominational status there was posed a question whether the child whose parents dropped the Church or the State-recognized religious union and whose parents declared being of non-denominational status, took over also the non-denominational status from his/her parents. The point was that at first the Administrative Tribunal was an advocate of the opinion which contradicted the liberal spirit of statutory law and which pronounced that – according to the Austrian legislation – each child had to be affiliated with one of the denominations which were recognized by the State. This meant that if the parents did not predetermine the denomination of their child, the administrative agencies could do that. While doing this, the agencies excercised their discretionary power and as a rule the child was classified to the Catholic millieu.

Such maneuvers of State organs contradicted the principle of *Rechtsstaat.* The latter required that imposing any legal duty on anybody should be based on the express statutory provision. This was the position adopted by the Administrative Tribunal when in 1882 it ruled that the child born to the parents who were of non-denominational status also acquired that status and consequently could obtain the upbringing that was indifferent to any religion. Such child consequently did not have to attend the religious instruction lessons at school.[4]

When before the last decade preceding the outbreak of World War I the process of leaving the Catholic Church by the Austrian citizens expressly intensified, the Austrian bureaucracy, while pressed by the governmental circles, attempted to restore the legal duty of providing religious instruction to children. The administrative authorities began to impose on non-denominational parents the duty to send their child to the lessons of the religion that was selected for him or her. The demand that a certain religion be selected for the child contradicted however the constitutional guarantee of freedom of religion and conscience. Nevertheless the Administrative Tribunal legitimated the activities of State agencies by introducing – beyond the *praeter legem* statute – the duty to take lessons in religion by non-denominational children.[5]

The problem consisted in this however that, despite the legal duty, imposed by the Administrative Tribunal decisions, to teach religion to non-denominational children, the parents of such children refused to comply with the administrative order commanding them to select some religion that the child would have to learn at school. The authorities threatened the parents with the execution of an administrative decision. The execution could be applied on the basis of the Patent of 1854. The Patent allowed to impose a fine or an arrest up to 14 days on those who refused to subordinate themselves to adminstrative orders.

In this situation the parents filed their complaint with the Constitutional Tribunal and raised an argument that the administrative decision in question provides for a religious coercion which is inadmissible since it contradicts the constitutional guarantee of freedom of religion and conscience. In its decision issued in 1914 the Constitutional Tribunal in fact held that the constitutional guarantee was infringed exactly because the administrative decision was safeguarded with the administrative-penal sanction. By doing this the Tribunal proved that it remained the guardian of the Constitution also in the era when the liberal spirit of December Constitution was partly being abandoned.

The second of the discussed Administrative Tribunal decisions was the one in which certain symptoms of clericalism within the State structures were detectable. The case that laid foundations for the decision in question referred to the legal basis of contributions paid for the benefit of Church institutions. In its decisions the Administrative Tribunal awarded to each taxpayer in the specific Commune the right to file a complaint against the Commune authorities' decisions referring to the subsidies for the benefit of denominational institutions.

In the early period of its activities the Tribunal fully respected the liberal nature of the Austrian statutory law that was adopted in the era when the constitutional order of the monarchy was being shaped. Therefore when the non-Catholic tax-payer demanded that the finances of the Church-building Committee be not subsidized out of the funds of the Commune, the Tribunal would quash the Commune decision referring to such subsidizing.

---

[4] *Idem, Orzecznictwo austriackiego Trybunału Administracyjnego w sprawach wyznaniowych (1876–1918)*, "Czasopismo Prawno-Historyczne", vol. XLVII, 1995, z. 1–2, p. 128.

[5] *Idem, Religionszwang ohne gesetzliche Grundlage? Interkonfesionelle Verhältnisse der Rechtsprechung des Österreichischen Verwaltungsgerichtshofes 1876-1918. Zeitschrift für Neuere Rechtsgeschichte*, 19. Jahrgang 1997, no. 1–2, p. 78.

                                                                    Andrzej Dziadzio

Thus for a long time, on the basis of the 1868 law and the principle of separation of the Church from the State as derived therefrom, the Tribunal adopted a view that the decisions on allocating the Commune funds for denominational goals of the Catholic Church were illegal. When in 1900 the Administrative Tribunal faced yet again the question of legality or illegality of the Commune subsidy for the purpose of erecting a parish church, the successor to the throne allegedly intervened in the decision-making process via the President of the Tribunal. Despite the successor's express suggestion that the Tribunal should consent to the Commune's request and not to that of the complaining tax-payers, the Tribunal resisted the pressure exerted on it by the Court circles. They say that the attitude of the Tribunal's President who did not knuckle down to the pressure of the Court of the Emperor resulted in the complaint that Francis Ferdinand was supposed to lodge with the Emperor, the complaint being tantamount to the pronouncement: "in Austria one is no longer allowed to erect churches".[6] The Emperor indeed took sides with the Tribunal's President and – they say – admonished the successor to the throne by arguing that the ruler could not interfere in the matters subjected to independent courts, but nevertheless quite soon the Administrative Tribunal began to change its decisions in the discussed area into such that were advantageous for the Communes. The Tribunal classified the decisions relating to the allowances for the Church institutions as those that lay within the scope of free administration of the Communal property. What was sufficient for considering such decisions legal was the raising of an argument that invoked the general social interest as the justification of the subsidy. The requirements of the concept of general social interest were deemed to have been fulfilled if the purposes other than the denominational ones were indicated. Thus the church could be built out of the Communal funds if its erection was, for instance, designed to honor the succession of the Emperor to the throne, the erection being then regarded as a patriotic act. The change in the nature of decisions made by the Administrative Tribunal showed that the latter surrendered to the expectations of the bureaucracy which, at the final stage of the Austrian monarchy, operated in the ever more clerical spirit.

The Role Played by the Constitutional Tribunal in Preserving the Liberal Nature of the Habsburg Monarchy at the Turn of the 19th Century

Summary

In the second part of the 19th century the Austrian monarchy was exponential of the series of features that were characteristic of the *Rechtsstaat*. In compliance with a series of Constitutional Laws that were referred to as the December Constitution of 1867, the monarchy guaranteed the observance of significant civil rights. The institutions that

---

[6] T. Olechowski, *Die Einfürung der Verwaltungsgerichtsbarkeit in Österreich*, Wien 1999, p. 232.

secured the implementation of the latter were the Tribunals of public law: the Constitutional Tribunal (*Reichsgericht*), the Administrative Tribunal (*Verwaltungsgerichtshof*) and the Tribunal of State (*Staatsgerichtshof*). Particularly the Constitutional Tribunal safeguarded the Constitution by examining the complaints filed by the citizens against the State agencies' infringements of the Constitution-guaranteed basic rights. While resorting to the analysis of specific controversial cases, the present paper tries to show to what extent the Constitutional Tribunal but also the Administrative Tribunal had their share in supporting the image of Austria as the *Rechtsstaat*. The author of the paper emphasizes that this was not an easy task to carry out. On one side there were observable the growing libertarian, nationalistic, modernist and socialdemocratic tendencies, very hostile toward the traditional State and the Church. On the other side there was detectable the consolidation of clerical tendencies in the Emperor's Court circles that tried to exert a pressure on the Tribunals. This rendered the keeping of balance between the two tendencies ever more difficult.

Eszter Cs. Herger

„Freie Kirche im freien Staat": Die katholische Autonomiebewegung in Ungarn

Die Kirche ist zu keiner Form der Gesellschaft oder des Staates gebunden, und je mehr unabhängig ist, je mehr keiner Unterstützung der Macht bedarf, umso eher stark ist.[1]

Die Kirchenverfassung und die Autonomie

Die Autonomie ist eine eigene Rechtsetzung, eine Freiheit der dem Staat unterworfenen Rechtsperson. Sie bedeutet die Möglichkeit zur Bestimmung der obligatorischen inneren Rechtsnormen. Man versteht darunter auch Selbstregierung oder Selbstverwaltung, die Berechtigung der autonomen Rechtsperson zur Verwaltung ihrer eigener Angelegenheiten. Im Falle der Kirchen ist die Autonomie einerseits eine Art der Verbindung der Kirche zu dem Staat: Die Selbstgesetzgebung und die Selbstverwaltung sind vom Staat unabhängige, doch durch den Staat „verliehene" innere Rechte, die vom öffentlichen Recht geregelt und begrenzt sind. Anderseits bedeutet sie auch die partikulare Selbstverwaltung der Kirchenmitglieder innerhalb der allgemeinen Autonomie. Diese Institution ist aber nicht durch das Verfassungsrecht geregelt, sondern sie ist überwiegend infolge des eigenartigen Aufbaus der Kirche zustande gekommen oder weggefallen und sie steht auf theologischen Gründen. Der kanonische *Autonomiebegriff* geht nicht vom Verhältnis zwischen Kirche und Staat, sondern von der Souveränität der Kirche aufgrund des göttlichen Rechts (ius Divinum) aus. Die Autonomie ist so eine selbstverständliche Berechtigung der universalen Kirche gegenüber dem Staat.

In der letzten Periode des römischen Imperiums und in den Jahrhunderten nach dem Untergang des West-römischen Reiches war die Autonomie der „Reichskirche" (380) bzw. der „Eigenkirchen" der katholisierten germanischen Fürstentümer verehrt, solange sie die Souveränität der weltlichen Macht nicht verletzte. Die hohe Geistlichkeit war die erste Gruppe der Gesellschaft, die um ihre Interesse zu verfechten und zur Geltung

---

[1] Győző Choncha, *Eötvös és Montalembert barátsága. Adalékok a magyar katholikusok autonómiájához* [Die Freundschaft von Eötvös und Montalembert. Erläuterungen zur Autonomie der ungarischen Katholiken], Budapest 1918, S. 179.

zu bringen einheitlich auftrat und sich zum Stand organisierte: Die Hochpriester, die
zur Zeit der Ständemonarchie durchgehends bedeutende politische und gesellschaftliche
Macht verfügten, waren – der Meinung von Thomas von Aquin nach – berechtigt, über
die weltliche Herrschaft ein moralisches Urteil zu sprechen. Vom 16. Jahrhundert an
erschien die Souveränität des von kirchlichen Gebundenheiten befreiten Herrschers in
den westlichen Staaten. Seine Befugnisse vermehrten sich gegenüber der Kirche durch
den Ausbau der absoluten königlichen Macht. Um die staatliche Souveränität zu sichern
strebte er nach dem Zurückdrängen des päpstlichen Einflusses und nach der Geltendmachung des weltlichen Charakters der absoluten Herrschaftsform. Die Freiheit eines
christlichen Herrschers bedeutete keine unbeschränkte Macht, sondern das ius Divinum begrenzte auch weiterhin seine Machtausübung. Doch war nicht nur die kirchliche eigene Rechtssetzung, sondern auch die Freiheit der kirchlichen Selbstverwaltung
beschädigt. Der Anspruch auf eine moderne Autonomie erschien erstmal zur Zeit der
bürgerlichen Umgestaltung in diejenigen Staaten, wo die katholische Kirche durch die
Entstehung einer protestierten Nationalkirche (Church of England, 1534, Religionsfriede
bei Augsburg, 1555) die Kirche der religiösen Minderheit wurde, wo durch die radikale Säkularisierung und Entrechtung der bisherigen Staatskirche (Frankreich, 1789), wo
durch die Sicherung der persönlichen und kollektiven Glaubensfreiheit und der Gleichberechtigung der Kirchen („Denominationalismus", 1. Zusatzartikel der Verfassung der
Vereinigten Staaten von Amerika, 1791) oder wo durch den Verlust der staatskirchlichen
Rechtsstellung (Ungarn, 1848) die mächtigere staatliche Unterstützung verlor.

Die katholische Kirche machte Anspruch auf die Autonomie ihrer Kirchenprovinzen
von den Staaten, aber wies die partikulare Selbstverwaltung der Kirchenmitglieder ab.
Der theokratische und zentralisierte Charakter ihrer Struktur schloss es aus, dass man der
Kirche, einem vom Gott gegründetes Institut – als eine Ganzheit oder an einem politisch
oder geographisch umgrenzten Gebiet – eine Selbstverwaltung gemäß dem öffentlich-
rechtlichen Sinne des Wortes beilegen könnte. Infolge der päpstlichen Vollmacht und der
tief gegliederten hierarchischen Struktur ist der Besitzer der kirchlichen Macht der Klerus, und nicht die weltliche Mitglieder der Kirche. Eine kanonische Autonomie gebührte
den Kapiteln, den Mönchorden, aufgrund eines päpstlichen Privilegs den Universitäten
der Geistlichen und aufgrund eines bischöflichen Privilegs den religiösen Vereinen. Diese Rechte kamen den Geistlichen zu, mit Ausschließung der Weltlichen und natürlich in
hierarchischer Ordnung.

Die neuere Erläuterung der Autonomie erschien in der katholischen Kirche als eine
notgedrungene Formation. In Ungarn fing die katholische Autonomiebewegung 1848
wegen dem Verlust der staatskirchlichen Rechtsstellung und der Angst vor der Säkularisierung des Kirchenvermögens an. Es war ein weitläufiger, aber kein erfolgreicher Pro-
zess. Man verstand nun darunter „eine aktive Teilnahme der weltlichen Kirchenmitglieder in der Kirchenverwaltung (nämlich in der Rechtsetzung, in der Administration und in
der Vermögensverwaltung) und die nötige Organisation".[2] Die Teilnahme der weltlichen
Personen durfte sich nur auf die sog. äußeren Sachen beziehen: Die Autonomie bedeutet

---

[2] Emil Kumlik, *Katholikus egyházközségek önkormányzata különös tekintettel Pozsonyra. Jogtörténeti
és egyházpolitikai tanulmány* [Die Selbstverwaltung der katholischen Kirchengemeinden mit besonderer
Rücksicht auf Pozsony], Pozsony 1911, S. 3.

nicht die Separierung der autonomen Organisation von der römischen Kirche und die Jurisdiction des Papstes oder der Bischöfe darf dadurch keinen Schaden erleiden. Es war mit keinem Wort die Rede davon, dass sie eine Selbstverwaltung nach dem Muster der Protestanten wäre, und es bedeutete nicht die Aufgabe der Grundprinzipien über den Klerus.[3] Die katholische Autonomie war zur Zeit der Wende der 19/20. Jahrhunderte als ein Recht gegenüber den anderen Kirchen und dem Staat bzw. der städtischen Selbstverwaltung erläutert, was unter der Aufsicht des kompetenten Hochpriesters, der Hierarchie untergeordnet, funktioniert.[4]

In der Rechtsliteratur war es am Ende des 19. Jahrhunderts allgemein angenommen, dass

> auch die katholische Autonomie eine Vorgeschichte hat, die die wissenschaftliche Begründung der Selbstverwaltung der Laien gegenüber der theologisch-kanonischen Argumentierung verstärken kann.

Während Thomas von Aquin die kirchliche Macht auf zwei Teilen geteilte, spricht das moderne Kanonrecht[5] über *potestas magisterii*, *potestas ministerii* und *potestas iurisdictionis*. Das Prinzip des universalen Priestertums der Gläubiger ist von der katholischen Geschichtsschreibung auch in Hinsicht der Urkirche unerkannt,[6] und sie wies alle Muster der Protestanten ab. Gemäß der monarchischen und hierarchischen Kirchenverfassung haben die Laien keinen Teil von der kirchlichen Macht, ihre eventuellen Rechte zur Vermögensverwaltung oder in Hinsicht der Ernennung der kirchlichen Würdenträger können nur als Verpflichtung erklärt werden. So ist die Institution des Patronatsrechts dem Wesen nach die einzige allgemeine Möglichkeit der Gläubiger, wodurch sie die kirchliche Machtausübung einfließen können.

Das Patronatsrecht des ungarischen Königs (*ius patronatus regiae majestatis*)[7] erschien zugleich als *eine nationale Autonomie* mit monarchischem Charakter innerhalb der universalen Kirchenorganisation, obwohl die katholische Kirche ein zentralisiertes Institut ist, was gemäß der offiziellen Auffassung nicht aus nationalen Kirchen, sondern aus Teilkirchen besteht.

Das *universalum ecclesiarum regni patronus*, ein subsidiares Recht, bedeutete die Berechtigung des Königs, wenn ein Donationsgut an ihn zurückfiel bzw. die Missbräuche des Patrons oder die Interesse des Landes es benötigten.

---

[3] Die theoretische Gründe der katholischen Autonomie siehe bei Wilhelm Emmanuel Freiherrn von Ketteler, *Freiheit, Autorität und Kirche. Erörterungen über die großen Probleme der Gegenwart*, Mainz 1862, S. 156–185 und Emil Friedberg, *Lehrbuch des katholischen und evangelischen Kirchenrechts*, Leipzig 1909, S. 71–87 und 110–120.

[4] Kumlik (Anm. 2), S. 16.

[5] *Codex Iuris Canonici*, Budapest 1995, c. 747 und 834.

[6] Zur Entstehung der örtlichen und Missionshierarchie siehe Konrád Szántó, *A katolikus egyház története* [Die Geschichte der katholischen Kirche], Budapest 1983, S. 56–65, zur Frage der Kirchenorganisation in den 2–3. Jahrhunderten im gleichen Werk, S. 104–135.

[7] Das *ius patronatus regiae majestatis* war in der Gemeinsprache *patronatus regium* genannt. Siehe: Ferenc Csorba, *A királyi kegyúri jog igaz mivolta* [Die wahre Beschaffenheit des königlichen Patronatsrechts], Budapest 1930, S. 25.

Das *ius patronatus* war eine Berechtigung und Verpflichtung einer natürlichen Person oder einer Rechtsperson, die sie wegen besonderer Verdienste (im Allgemeinen wegen Kirchenbau) verschaffte.[8] In Ungarn war das Kirchengebäude im Besitz des Adeligen (*ecclesia sua, monasterium suum, clastrum suum*) und das Patronatsrecht war ein Teil des Nachlasses, man konnte es verkaufen oder verpfänden. Vom 13. Jahrhundert an erschien das Patronatsrecht der Ansiedlergemeinden (Hospesgemeinden) bzw. der Städte als eine Freiheit aufgrund königlicher Privilegien.[9] Das *ius patronatus der Grundbesitzer und der Städte* lebte weite bis zur modernen Zeit, und führte zu neueren Problemen: Oft forderten auch die nicht katholischen Bewohner das Recht zum Wahlen der kirchlichen Würdenträger. Die katholische Elite und der hohe Klerus hofften am Ende des 19. Jahrhunderts, dass die einheitliche Regelung der kirchlichen Autonomie auch diesen Gegensatz beseitigen kann.

Ein einzigartiges Beispiel der Selbstverwaltung der Laien war *der sog. katholische Status in Siebenbürgen*.[10] Die protestierten Stände vernichteten 1556 das katholische Bistum und sein Vermögen wurde säkularisiert. Der Einfluss der weltlichen Kirchenmitglieder auf die kirchlichen Sachen kam infolge dieser Zwangslage zustande.[11] Zur Zeit des Neoabsolutismus (1849–1867) war der Status fast vernichtet, er bekam aber eine volle Anerkennung 1918 (*Codex Iuris Canonici*, c. 1521).[12]

Die erste katholische Autonomiebewegung

Die ungarischen hohen Geistlichen meldeten ihren Anspruch auf den Ausbau der Autonomie erstmal im März 1848, als der letzte Ständetag über die Frage der Verbindung der Kirchen zum Staat verhandelte. Parallel zum Ständetag versammelte sich am 20. März auch das Episkopat im Pressburger Palast des Primas. Das wichtigste Ziel ihrer Beratung war, dass der Herrscher sich seine Rechte gemäß dem GA 1790:23 gegenüber der katholischen Kirche vorbehalten solle. Sie legten in ihrer *Denkschrift*[13] fest, dass diese persönlichen, unübertragbaren Rechte an die Kirche zurückfielen, wenn der König sie nicht ausübe. Sie baten um *die Einrichtung einer aus Geistlichen und Laizisten bestehenden Kommission* für die Ernennung der hohen geistlichen Würdenträger, die Verwaltung der religiösen Fonds und die Leitung der Schulen. Sie wollten dies nach §§ 10 und 12 des

---

[8] Die genaue Verpflichtungen und Rechte siehe bei Ferenc Kollányi, *A magán kegyúri jog hazánkban a középkorban* [Das Privatpatronatsrecht in unserer Heimat im Mittelalter], Budapest 1906, S. 195–196.

[9] Siehe bei Ákos Timon, *A városi kegyuraság Magyarországon* [Das Patronatsrecht der Städte in Ungarn], Budapest 1889.

[10] Die Vergleichung der Autonomie der Kirchengemeinden und des katholischen Status in Siebenbürgen siehe bei Kumlik (Anm. 2), S. 153–155.

[11] Ferenc Csorba, *Az erdélyi kath. Autonómiáról* [Über die katholische Autonomie in Siebenbürgen], Budapest 1897, Mihály Bochkor, *Az erdélyi katolikus autonómia* [Die katholische Autonomie in Siebenbürgen], Kolozsvár 1911.

[12] Ignác Kosutányi, *Egyházjog. A magyarországi egyházak alkotmánya és közigazgatása* [Kirchenrecht. Verfassung und Verwaltung der Kirchen in Ungarn], Kolozsvár 1906, S. 241–242.

[13] Mihály Fogarasy, *Emlékirat az 1847–48. országgyűlés alatt Pozsonyban tartott püspöki tanácskozmányokról egy résztvevőtől* [Denkschrift über die Beratungen des Episkopats in Pressburg zur Zeit des Ständetages 1847–48], Pest 1848.

GA 1790:26 in Form eines Selbstverwaltungsträgers einrichten. Es hätte somit nur zur Folge gehabt, dass der König das *ius patronatus* nicht durch das Ministerium, sondern durch die Kommission ausgeübt hätte, wenn er persönlich von diesem keinen Gebrauch gemacht hätte.[14]

GA 1848:3 über die Etablierung der selbstständigen verantwortlichen ungarischen Regierung und GA 1848:20 über den Glauben führten zur bedeutenden Veränderung in der Verbindung der Kirchen zum Staat. Der erste veränderte die Art der Ernennung der hohen geistlichen Würdenträger, der zweite deklarierte die Gleichberechtigung der gesetzlich anerkannten Kirchen und entschied über die staatliche Finanzierung der kirchlichen Schulen. Lajos Kossuth betrachtete die gesetzliche Regelung der katholischen Kirchenvermögen als eine Voraussetzung der Gleichberechtigung der Kirchen.[15] Im Interesse der Etablierung der selbstständigen Regierung und der Vernichtung der Lasten der Leibeigenen wollte er aber alle möglichen Konflikte umgehen: Der Gesetzgeber wählte die Variation „allen Kirchen und kirchlichen Schulen den gleichen materiellen Beitrag zu gewährleisten" statt „den Kirchen nichts zu geben".[16]

Die Verhandlungen des Gesetzesentwurfes über den Glauben fingen im Herrenhaus am 2. April 1848 an. János Scitovszky, Diözesanbischof von Pécs entwickelte seinen Standpunkt über „die wahre Bedeutung der Gleichberechtigung": Die Errichtung der katholischen Autonomie gemäß dem Muster der Protestanten(!) ist die wichtigste Voraussetzung der Gleichberechtigung. Mihály Fogarasy sprach auf „die Freiheit der Assotiation" berufend über die Unabhängigkeit der Kirche.[17] Die Bemerkungen der Bischöfe standen in Einklang mit den Zielsetzungen der Beratung des Episkopats. Sie sahen eine einzige Möglichkeit zur staatlichen Finanzierung der Schulen, und es war die Säkularisierung des Kirchenvermögens. So sie suchten den Weg um sie zu verhindern.

Der Anspruch auf die katholische Autonomie wurde erstmal in der Untertafel von Miklós Sárkány, Abt von Bakonybél am 4. April 1848 angemeldet. Kossuth bekannte, dass er ein gerechter Anspruch ist, wollte aber die gesetzliche Regelung dieser Frage auf später verschieben.[18]

Die Beratung des Episkopats, was mit Teilnahme angesehener katholischen Mitglieder des Ständetages stattfand, richtete sich in einer Adresse an Ferdinand V. am 6. April, und brachte eine Petition („Rónay-Petition") zum Ständetag am 7. April an. Die Rónay-Petition wurde von der Untertafel als „verspätete" untergelassen: Das Recht der Verwaltung über die Religions- und Schulfonds[19] wollte man nicht in Hand des Klerus geben,

---

[14] Veröffentlicht von Augustinus de Roskoványi (Hg.), *Monumenta Catholica pro Independentia Potestatis Ecclesiasticae ab Imperio Civil*, Pest 1856, Nr. 715, S. 362–366.

[15] László Csorba, *A szekularizáció kérdése a reformkori országgyűléseken* [Die Frage der Säkularisierung an den Ständetagen in der Reformzeit], Világosság 1979/10, S. 603–610.

[16] Ferenc Kossuth (Hg.), *Kossuth Lajos irata* [Die Schriften von Lajos Kossuth], Budapest 1900, Band VIII, S. 335.

[17] Die Verhandlungen des Herrenhauses siehe bei Árpád Zeller, *A magyar egyházpolitika 1847–1894* [Die Kirchenpolitik in Ungarn 1847–1894], Budapest 1894, S. 86–104.

[18] István Barta, *Kossuth Lajos az utolsó rendi országgyűlésen 1847–48* [Lajos Kossuth am letzten Ständetag 1847–1848], Budapest 1951, S. 727–728.

[19] Die Beratung siehe bei Erzsébet F. Kiss (Hg.), *Az 1848–1849. évi minisztertanácsi jegyzőkönyvek* [Protokolle des Ministerrates 1848–1849], Budapest 1989, S. 34.

der allgemein gegen die bürgerliche Umgestaltung Stellung nahm.[20] Der Primas rief die weltlichen Männer wieder zu einer Beratung am 8. April. Fogarasys Denkschrift nach ist der Gedanke *der Autonomie der Kirchengemeinden* erstmal hier aufgetaucht.[21]

Das neu errichtete Kulturministerium fing seine Arbeit mit der Führung von Baron József Eötvös.[22] Infolge des Mangels der gesetzlichen Regelung hing es persönlich von ihm und von der Regierung, was für ein Kompetenzbereich man dem Kulturministerium zueignet. Die nicht wirtschaftlichen und administrativen Fragen der kirchlichen Pfründe und Fonds gehörten der katholischen Abteilung, aber die Abteilung für Wirtschaft und Fonds beschäftigte sich mit allen ökonomischen Sachen.[23]

Im September 1848 flieh Eötvös nach Ausland. Der Diözesanbischof von Csanád und neue Kulturminister, Mihály Horváth rief in seiner Verordnung von 15. Juni 1849[24] die von weltlichen Kirchenmitgliedern gemäß der Anordnung der Regierung gewählten Vertreter der katholischen Kirche in Pest zu einer Beratung. Wegen den Ereignissen des Verteidigungskrieges bestand es aber keine Möglichkeit zur Abhaltung des Autonomiekongresses und die Frage der katholischen Autonomie wurde von der Tagesordnung abgesetzt.[25]

Die Frage der katholischen Autonomie zwischen 1849 und 1867

Die Zeit des Neoabsolutismus war auch von Hinsicht der Autonomiebewegung sehr ungünstig. Art. 2. der oktroyierten Märzverfassung ließ die bisherigen Gesetze und Verordnungen über die Religions- und Schulfonds in Kraft. Die gesetzlich anerkannten Kirchen jedoch durften ihre Angelegenheiten *frei und selbstständig verwalten*. Die Beratungen zwischen Episkopat und der österreichischen Regierung fanden vom 30. April bis 17. Juni 1849 in Wien unter der Leitung von Herzog Schwarzenberg, dem Erzbischof von Salzburg, statt. An den Beratungen nahm auch der ungarische Fürstprimas Scitovszky teil. *Im kaiserlichen Patent vom 18. April 1850* zum Vollzug der der katholischen Kirche verbürgten Rechte war es mit keinem Wort die Rede von der kirchlichen Autonomie.[26] Ungarn gehörte tatsächlich dem Geltungsbereich dieses Patents an. Die Teilnehmer der Konferenz des ungarischen Episkopats in Esztergom (25. August 1850) verfassten ihre Glückwünsche in ihrer Begrüßungsadresse, betonten die Rolle der „über die Kronen des Herrschers" wachenden Geistlichen und bekannten sich „zu der einen und untrennbaren Habsburgermonarchie". Sie drückten aber auch ihren Wunsch aus, dass das Patronats-

---

[20] Andor Csizmadia, *Az állam és az egyház kapcsolatai 1848/49-ben* [Verbindung der Kirche zu dem Staat 1848/49], Világosság 1981/8–9, S. 503, Árpád Zeller (Anm. 17), S. 165 und Ferenc Hanuy, *Hetven éves küzdelem az autonomiáért* [Ein 70 jähriger Kampf um die Autonomie], Budapest 1918, S. 9.

[21] Fogarasy (Anm. 13), S. 22.

[22] Die Tätigkeit von Eötvös siehe bei Andor Csizmadia, *Eötvös József egyházpolitikája* [Kirchenpolitik von József Eötvös], Világosság 1981/7, S. 437–446.

[23] Siehe weitere bei Erzsébet F. Kiss (Hg.), *Az 1848–1849-es magyar minisztériumok* [Die ungarischen Ministerien 1848–1849], Budapest 1987, S. 443.

[24] Den Text der Verordnung siehe bei Emil Szemnecz, *Katholikus autonómia* [Katholische Autonomie], Band I, Budapest 1897, S. 21–22.

[25] K. Dániel Keményfy, *Ötven év alkotm. Egyházpolitikája* [Verfassungsmäßige Kirchenpolitik von fünfzig Jahren], Esztergom 1898, S. 61–62.

[26] Veröffentlicht von Zeller (Anm. 17), S. 196–199.

recht des apostolischen Herrschers durch die veränderten Verhältnisse in Form eines Konkordats neu geregelt werden sollte. Das (am 18. August 1855 zwischen Franz Josef und Papst Pius IX. geschlossene) österreichische *Konkordat* führte mehrere Veränderungen ein, die den Gedanke der Autonomie langsam einschläferten, und die Bewegung war ohne Grund geblieben. Das Programm der Integration zu einem neoabsolutistischer Gesamtmonarchie erstreckte sich auch auf die kirchenpolitischen Fragen. In Interesse der Zentralisation zielte Franz Josef auf die Abschaffung der vorher selbstständigen landeskirchlichen Organisationen ab. Eine ideologische Bestätigung suchte der Herrscher demzufolge im Konkordat vom Jahre 1855, dessen „Preis" der Verlust eines erheblichen Teiles des königlichen Patronatsrechts war. Franz Josef erkannte voll und ganz das privilegium fori an, überließ die Verwaltung des Kirchenvermögens und seine Belastung von der päpstlichen Stellungnahme abhängig, überließ den Religions- und Studienfonds der kirchlichen Verwaltung, verzichtete auf einen Teil des Ernennungsrechts.[27]

Nach der Veröffentlichung des Oktoberdiploms (20. Oktober 1860) wurde die regierende Macht durch die Widererrichtung der ungarischen königlichen Hofkanzlei und des königlichen Statthalterrates so ausgeübt, wie bevor der Revolution. Bis zum österreichisch-ungarischen Ausgleich (1867) blieb die einzigartige Rechtsstellung der katholischen Kirche unverletzt, ohne Rücksicht auf den GA 1848:20. Das Episkopat richtete sich im Interesse der Errichtung einer kirchlichen Hofkommission mehrmals in Adresse an Franz Josef.[28] 1865 bekamen sie keine Antwort, 1866 wurde ihre Bitte abgewiesen: Aufgrund der Prinzip der Rechtskontinuität sollten die apostolischen Rechte des Königs so ausgeübt werden, wie es im GA 1848:3 bestimmt war.

Trotz diesen Schwierigkeiten erlosch die Autonomiebewegung zur Zeit des Neoabsolutismus nicht, sondern verlegte sich auf eine theoretische Ebene. József Eötvös schickte sein Werk „A XIX. század uralkodó eszméinek befolyása az álladalomra" („Einfluss der vorherrschenden Ideen des 19. Jahrhunderts auf den Staat") dem französischen Montalembert 1853, dessen Schrift „Freie Kirche im freien Staat"[29] das Bekenntnis der liberalen Katholiken in Ungarn wurde. In seinem Brief von 5. Mai 1867 fasste Eötvös seine Meinung über die kirchliche Autonomie zusammen: „Es ist mir meine feste Überzeugung – in der mich Ihre so ausgezeichneten Schriften und Reden noch mehr bestärken – dass das Einzige was der Staat in unserem Jahrhundert für die Kirche thun kann, das Einzige dessen sie vom Staate bedarf das ist: dass ihr die vollste Freiheit gesichert werde."[30]

---

[27] Den ungarischen Text des Konkordats siehe in: *Az Austriai Concordatum fölvilágosítása* [Die Erklärung des österreichischen Konkordats], Pest 1856, S. 118–134.

[28] Gábor Salacz, *Egyház és állam Magyarországon a dualizmus korában 1867–1918* [Kirche und Staat in Ungarn zur Zeit des Dualismus 1867–1918], München 1974, S. 16.

[29] Das Werk von Montalembert erschien in Ungarn erstmal im Jahre 1864 in der Übersetzung von Pál Matkovits.

[30] Die 19 französischen und die 12 deutschen Briefe aus ihrem Briefwechsel sind veröffentlicht von Győző Choncha, *Eötvös és Montalembert barátsága. (Adalék a magyar katholikusok autonómiájának kezdeteihez)* [Die Freundschaft von Eötvös und Montalembert. Erläuterungen zur Autonomie der ungarischen Katholiken], Budapest 1918, Anhang, 7. Brief, Pest, den 5. Mai 1867.

Die zweite katholische Autonomiebewegung

Nach der Krönung von Franz Josef veränderten sich die kirchenpolitischen Verhältnisse
kaum. Eötvös, wieder als Kulturminister berief sich jetzt nicht auf das Schlagwort „freie
Kirche im freien Staat", sondern *auf die Bitte der Katholiken von Siebenbürgen.* Ihre
Beratung fand seit 1866 nicht statt, so er bat den König um die direkte Anordnung des
Bischofs von Siebenbürgen zum Zusammenrufen der katholischen „Stände". In seinem Brief von 20. Juni 1867 zum Primas János Simor entwickelte er seinen Standpunkt
über die Rechtsgleichheit: Die katholische Autonomie in Ungarn muss aufgrund dem
Muster der katholischen Status in Siebenbürgern zustande gebracht werden. Er forderte
die Errichtung der Selbstverwaltung und die vollste Freiheit der Katholiken, wie sie die
ungarische Protestanten seit Jahrhunderten hatten.[31]
János Simor verwies in seiner Antwort (8. September 1867) auf die ernste Entscheidung des Episkopats, die in den Adressen zu dem König schon zweimal erörtert war.
Im nächsten Monat versammelten sich die Hochpriester in Buda um die Rahmen der
Autonomie zu bestimmen. Der Entwurf wurde mit den führenden weltlichen Katholiken
mitgeteilt. Die Beauftragten der Bischofskonferenz fingen ihre Arbeit am 24. Juni 1869
an, und sie nahmen am 26. September 1869 den Entwurf über den Einfluss der weltlichen Katholiken an, der aber – Eötvös' Meinung zitierend – „so engherzig" geschaffen
war, dass die Weltlichen und die niedere Geistlichkeit dagegen Stellung nahmen.[32] Am
Jahresschluss setzte Eötvös große Hoffnungen auf die Vorbereitungen:

> (…) So hoffte ich noch im Jahre 869, so Gott mir das Leben schenkt, alle kirchlichen Gemeinschaf-
> ten Ungarns autonom organisiert zu sehen und dadurch den Grundsatz der freien Kirche im freien
> Staate endlich wenigstens in einem Lande durchzuführen, nachdem hierzu vor Allem notwendig
> ist, dass dem Staate nicht bloß Individuen verschiedener Religion, sondern organisierte Kirchenge-
> meinden entgegen stehen.[33]

Der I. Kongress tagte von 26. Oktober 1870 bis 30. März 1871.[34] Inzwischen ver-
schied József Eötvös, und ohne ihn kamen die Verhandlungen noch langsamer vorwärts.
Das endlich angenommene Statut (1871)[35] deduzierte das Recht zur Autonomie der weltlichen und geistlichen Kirchenmitglieder aus dem Gleichberechtigungsprinzip des Gesetzartikels 1848:20. Das *summum ius patronatus* des Königs wurde unverletzt bewahrt.
Das übersichtliche, logische Statut bestimmte drei Stufen der Organisation. Neben der
Landesversammlung, der Komitatsversammlung und der Gemeindeversammlung stan-

---

[31] A főmélt. Hercegprímás három irata [Drei Schriften des Primas], Pest 1867, S. 40.

[32] Choncha (Anm. 30) Anhang, 9. Brief, Pest, 20. Juni 1868.

[33] *Idem* (Anm. 30) Anhang, 11. Brief, Pest, 15. Dezember 1868.

[34] Die Verhandlungen siehe bei Antal Günther (Hg.), *A magyarországi latin és görög szertartású katho-
likus egyház önkormányzatát szervező gyűlés naplója, jegyzőkönyvei s irományai* [Tagebuch, Protokolle und
Schriften der die kirchliche Selbstverwaltung der ungarischen Katholiken organisierenden Versammlung],
Band I–II, Pest 1871.

[35] Günther (Hg.) (Anm. 34), *A magyarországi latin és görög szertartású katholikusok egyházi önkor-
mányzatának szervezete: A kath. cong. által 1871. mártius 29-én harmadszori olvasás után elfogadott szöveg*
[Die Organisation der kirchlichen Selbstverwaltung der römischen und griechischen Katholiken in Ungarn:
Der am 29. März 1871, nach der dritten Lesung vom kath. Kongress angenommene Text], Band II, Nr. 15.

den Exekutivorgane, der sog. Direktionsrat, der Komitatsrat und endlich der Rat der Kirchengemeinde.

Während der Vorbereitung des Statuts gang eine starke Debatte im Abgeordnetenhaus über *die rechtliche Natur der Religions- und Schulfonds,* besser gesagt über die eventuellen vermögensrechtlichen Folgen der Autonomie. Infolge der Diskussion[36] wurde eine Kommission beauftragt um eine rechtshistorische Analyse über den Ursprung dieser Fonds vor dem Abgeordnetenhaus zu bringen.[37] Das vom katholischen Kongress angenommene Statut wurde vom König nicht sanktioniert, sondern Tivadar Pauler zugeschickt, aber der neue Kulturminister, der in religiösen Fragen besonders konservative Stellung vertrat, machte nichts für Interesse der Erfolg.

Am 17. Februar 1886 stellte Ágost Trefort, der Nachfolger von Pauler an der Spitze des Kulturministeriums, einen Antrag auf die Errichtung der örtlichen Selbstverwaltungen in seinem Brief zu dem Episkopat.[38] In den Städten, wo die Bevölkerung aus religiöser Hinsicht gemischt war, war es fraglich, ob die Nichtkatholiken Recht zur Wahl der Geistlichen haben. Die Etablierung der kirchlichen Selbstverwaltungen in den Städten hätte diese Debatte beruhigend befriedigen können. Am Anfang der 90-er Jahre war es eine allgemeine Stellungnahme in der Reihe der politischen Elite, dass die katholische Autonomie *von unten nach oben* ausgebaut werden muss.

Trotz der Bestrebung der katholischen Intelligenz kam es zwischen 1871 und 1895 zu keiner wesentlichen Fortschritt. Die Zielsetzung des Episkopats veränderte sich nicht, doch es waren mehrere äußeren Schwierigkeiten – wie es Hanuy behauptete.[39] Die passive Haltung der griechisch-katholischen Rumäner und die Debatte über den Ursprung und rechtlichen Natur der Religions- und Schulfonds beeinflussten die Bewegung ungünstig. Den größten Zweifel erweckte der Artikel 4. des Statuts vom Jahre 1871: Der Eigentümer allen kirchlichen Vermögens war diesem Artikel nach die Gesamtheit der Katholiken und nicht die kirchliche Rechtspersonen.

Die Modernisierung der Verbindung der Kirchen zu dem Staat war ein wichtiger Teil der politischen Zielsetzungen der Szapáry- und der Wekerle-Regierung zur Zeit der sog. *zweiten liberalen Welle des 19. Jahrhunderts* in Ungarn. Die Frage der katholischen Autonomie blieb aber aus der Reihe der Reformgesetze[40] weg. Aufgrund des Antrags der Regierung bewilligte der König das Zusammenrufen des II. Autonomiekongresses am 29. November 1895. Nach den Wahlen der Vertreter im Sommer 1897 wurde der Kongress am 11. November eröffnet. Es gab vier verschiedene Konzeptionen bzw. Parteien. Der Episkopat befürwortete eine solche Autonomie, die die kirchliche Hierarchie nicht berührt. Der freisinnigen Regierung, den mittleren Adeligen und den niederen Geistlichen gelang es eine gemeinsame Plattform zu finden. Die konservativen Magnaten konzentrierten auf die Ausgabe der Religiösen- und Schulfonds, und endlich muss auch

---

[36] Zitiert von Zeller (Anm. 17), S. 601–615.

[37] *Idem* (Anm. 17), S. 625–629.

[38] Zitiert von Kumlik (Anm. 2), S. 173.

[39] Hanuy (Anm. 20), S. 25.

[40] GA 1894:31 über die Zivilehe, GA 1894: 32 über den Glauben der aus gemischten Ehen geborenen Kinder, GA 1894:33 über die staatliche Matrikelführung, GA 1895:42 über die Emanzipation der Israeliten und GA 1895:43 über die Glaubensfreiheit.

die radikale Minderheit erwähnt werden, die die Autonomie aufgrund des katholischen Status in Siebenbürgen vorstellten.

Die 27 Mitglieder der Vorbereitungskommission beendeten ihre Arbeit am Anfang 1900. Der Entwurf war schon mehrmals durchgearbeitet und auch die radikalen Mitglieder der Kommission machten ihren eigenen Entwurf fertig. Die Kongressverhandlungen fingen nur am 9. Januar 1902 an, und der definitive Vorschlag wurde an der Abschlusssitzung vom 10. März 1902 angenommen. Für Hinsicht der Religions- und Schulfonds war es wichtig, dass der Kongress seinen Standpunkt in einer *Erklärung über den Rechtsvorbehalt* festlegte. Die wissenschaftliche Debatte über den Ursprung und über die rechtliche Natur dieser Fonds von zwei Jahrzehnten vor Augen haltend wand der Statutentwurf eine überbrückende Lösung an: Die autonome Organe bekamen nur Aufsichtsrecht (§§ 164–171) und ein enges Verfügungsrecht (§ 167 und § 169), das Recht zur Verwaltung blieb aber im Kompetenzbereich des zuständigen Ministers (§ 11).

Der Geltungsbereich des Statutentwurfs erstreckte sich auch auf die griechischen Katholiken. Er betraf den katholischen Status von Siebenbürgen nicht. Der Status hatte eine Möglichkeit in die ungarische Autonomie mit Zustimmung der Landessitzung einzugliedern (§ 7). Die katholische Autonomie war im Entwurf auch dadurch verengert, dass er das Oberpatronatsrecht des „apostolischen" ungarischen Königs (*summum ius patronatus*) und das Oberaufsichtsrecht überhaupt nicht berührte (§ 2).

Gegenüber dem Statutsentwurf vom Jahre 1871, ließ der zweite Entwurf das Eigentumsrecht der Bistümer, der Kapitel bzw. der Körperschaften und der Rechtspersonen auf die von ihnen verwalteten Stiftungen und Fonds unverletzt. Eine der wichtigsten Fragen des Kongresses war den richtigen Weg zwischen Zentralisierung und Dezentralisierung zu finden. Am zweiten Autonomiekongress wurde der Schwerpunkt der autonomen Organe auf die Landesversammlung und dessen Exekutivorgan, auf den Direktionsrat verlegt.

Die vom Kongress gewählte Deputation gab die Adresse, den Statutentwurf und die Erklärung über den Rechtsvorbehalt dem König am 13. März 1902 über. Franz Josef schickte diese Schriften dem Kulturminister Wlassics weiter. Der Minister bereitete die Antwort des Herrschers vor, der dann um die Meinungsäußerung des Episkopats bat. *Die ungarische Hochpriester antworteten aber nur nach mehr als vier Jahren*, am 2. September 1906. Hanuy wusste über die geheimen Verhandlungen der nächsten elf Jahren nichts, es ist aber wohl bekannt, dass ein Gesetzesentwurf über die katholische Autonomie schon bevor 1910 ausgearbeitet war. Die politischen Ereignisse und die Gegensätze zwischen den Parteien führten aber dazu, dass *die erste Gesetzesvorlage nur am 21. Dezember 1917, zur Zeit des ersten Weltkriegs vor dem Parlament eingebracht wurde*. Diese Vorlage erwies sich aber ohne Erfolg gebliebene, und die katholische Autonomiebewegung in Ungarn wurde damit von der Tagesordnung endgültig abgesetzt.

"Free Church in a Free State": The Movement of Catholic Autonomy in Hungary in the 19th Century

Summary

Legal historians and those dealing with the history of society and Church alike take an interest in modernization in the 19th century, including the harmonization of the legal relationship between the Hungarian state and Churches with the principles of the development of a civil state. This is why this issue has been the topic of numerous works since the dualistic era (1867–1918). Referring to western, mainly American and French examples, the liberal political elite in the reform period and later the liberal thinkers in the dualistic era urged modernization concerning Church affairs in their writings and parliamentary speeches. However, the issue of catholic autonomy got primarily on the agenda due to the influence of the Hungarian episcopate and the devoted liberal Catholic intelligentsia following the so called April Laws of 1848: losing the status of state Church and fears of the secularization of property triggered the long-lasting but not very fruitful autonomy movement the followers of which considered autonomy as active participation of temporal believers in the Church government and the legal organization effecting it. In their view temporal participation, which was regarded as an obligation and not as a right, could exclusively relate to the so called external matters (asset handling, education, patronage and Church protection) and neither the separation of the organization from the Roman Church nor injury to the papal and episcopal jurisdiction was meant by it. The movement enjoyed support in respect of principles rather than in respect of its implementation. The study below endeavours to describe the causes which gave rise to it and the partial results it could achieve between 1848 and 1918 emphasizing that in the case of any Churches an autonomous organization may only be developed if both the relationship between the state and the given Church and the internal nature of the Church urge autonomy.

ISTVÁN KAJTÁR

Prof. Andor Csizmadia Dr. Dr. h.c. and His Research into the Legal History of Dualism

Professor Andor Csizmadia (1910–1985) is renowned as one of the most outstanding figures of Hungarian legal history in the second part of the 20th century.[1] There are two well-established reasons for dealing with his scientific career rich in achievements at the conference on "The Constitutional system of the Habsburg monarchy in the last decades before its fall. The search for the elements of Rechtsstaat" held in Krakow within the framework of the co-operation between the Departments of Legal History of the Universities of Pécs and Krakow on 22–26 October 2007. On the one hand, Andor Csizmadia was doctor honoris causa of the Jagiellonian University. On the other hand, his studies presenting the findings in his main fields of research are always intertwined with the analysis of the constitutional and legal history of dualism. It follows that the many-sided evaluation of his research into the dualistic era would be impossible without first gaining some insight into his life achievement.

It should be noted that Hungarian law applied the principle of legal continuity in 1919–1944, consequently the late dualistic law formed a substantial part of the law in effect in the first part of the 20th century – thus Csizmadia, the future legal historian, as a civil servant applied the effective law which he later studied as public administration and law of the past and described in its historical context. Andor Csizmadia filled in positions in central social administration after 1945. Later he moved into higher education, he obtained a qualification as an honorary lecturer at the Technical University of

---

[1] On his life achievement: Ádám Antal, *Csizmadia Andor 70 éves* [Andor Csizmadia is 70 years old], [in:] *Jogtörténeti tanulmányok: Emlékkönyv Csizmadia Andor hetvenedik születésnapjára* [Studies on the history of law. Essays honoring Professor Andor Csizmadia on his 70th birthday], eds. Ádám Antal, Benedek Ferenc, Szita János, Pécs, PTE ÁJK, 1980. *Studia iuridica auctoritate Universitatis Pécs publicata 95.* pp.17–29; Kajtár István, *Csizmadia Andor (1910–1985)*, [in:] *Magyar jogtudósok* [Hungarian jurists]. ed. Hamza Gábor, Budapest 2001, pp.177–196. Bibliographies: *Csizmadia Andor tudományos munkássága.* Összeállította: Kajtár István [The scientific work of Andor Csizmadia. Compiled by István Kajtár], [in:] *Jogtörténeti tanulmányok: Emlékkönyv Csizmadia Andor hetvenedik születésnapjára* [Studies on the history of law. Essays honoring Professor Andor Csizmadia on his 70th birthday], pp. 423–432; *Csizmadia Andor (1910–1985). Szakmai bibliográfia. 1936–2003 között megjelent munkák.* Összeállította: Kajtár Istvánné. Andor Csizmadia (1910–1985). Professional bibliography. Works published in 1936–2003. Compiled by Istvánné Kajtár], [in:] *Jogtörténeti tanulmányok VIII.* [Studies on the history of law], eds. Béli Gábor, Kajtár István, Szekeres Róbert, Pécs 2005, PTK ÁJK, pp. 575–598.

Budapest, and then he was appointed a lecturer at the Academy of Law in Eger. He also delivered lectures at the Faculty of Economics of the Technical University of Budapest and later worked at the Department of Constitutional Law of the Faculty of Law of Eötvös Loránd University (ELTE) in Budapest. From 1958 to 1980 – up to his retirement – he was head of department of the Department of Legal History of the Faculty of Law of the University of Pécs. He was the Dean of the Faculty in 1964–1968. At the time of and around the six hundredth anniversary of the foundation of the university he contributed substantially to making our university well-known in Europe and to the enhancement of its good reputation. He received recognition several times: he was a corresponding member of the Austrian Academy of Sciences, doctor honoris causa of the Jagiellonian University of Krakow and was awarded the Golden Plaquette of the University of Vienna.

His life achievement is fascinating: more than three hundred books, studies, articles, publications of sources, reviews – and pieces of many other genres. In the beginning, his main fields of research were primarily of a constitutional-public administrative nature. Following a shift towards legal history in his scientific career, territorial, municipal and local-governmental legal history, the relationship between state and church, the issues of social administration, the development of the Hungarian public service, the history of government, the history of parliament and suffrage, the past of legal higher education and that of the discipline of legal history, and the issues relating to progressive legal traditions and the legal attitude of mind of outstanding statesmen got into the centre of his interest.

One-fifth of his work is made up of publications dealing with the legal history of the municipal and other territorial local-governments. Before 1945 the following should be regarded as important: *A magyar városi jog. Reformtörekvések a városi közigazgatásban*. [Hungarian municipal law. Reform endeavours in municipal administration] (1941).[2] Naturally, Csizmadia, who studied urban history, possessed an intimate knowledge of earlier historical periods as well. The analysis of the political efforts and endeavours of towns in the last decades of the dualistic era should be highlighted here: *A városi törvényhozás a dualizmus korában és az 1918. évi városi törvénytervezet* [Legislation on municipalities in the dualistic era and the bill on municipalities of 1918].[3] He also wrote about the typical co-ordinating organisations of dualistic public law, namely about the administrative committees operating in comitats (counties) and in towns with municipal rights and about communities, too.[4]

He was always interested in the relationship between state and church. *A magyar állam és az egyházak jogi kapcsolatainak kialakulása és gyakorlata a Horthy-korszakban*

---

[2] *A magyar városi jog. Reformtörekvések a városi közigazgatásban* [Hungarian municipal law. Reform endeavours in municipal administration], Kolozsvár, 1941, p. 227.

[3] *A városi törvényhozás a dualizmus korában és az 1918. évi városi törvénytervezet* [Legislation on municipalities in the dualistic era and the bill on municipalities of 1918], [in:] *Állam és Igazgatás*, 1982.11. sz-m, pp. 988–998.

[4] *A "közigazgatási bizottság" a polgári állam szervezetében* ["Administrative committees" in the bourgeois state organisation], [in:] *Jogtörténeti tanulmányok* II, Budapest 1968, pp. 117–138. *A községi jegyző jogállása és magánmunkálatainak értékelése a polgári korban* [The legal status of community notaries and the evaluation of their private workings in the bourgeois era], [in:] *Jogtörténeti tanulmányok* VI, Budapest 1986, pp. 81–95.

[The development of church-state legal relations in Hungary in the Horthy era][5] was produced as a synthesis. This work together with its German edition attracted special attention in scientific circles. Csizmadia dealt with this subject through his whole life with special regard to the dualistic era.

Many of his works deal with administration in general and with its history, due mainly to the impact of the years spent in public administration. His work submitted to competition in the field of the simplification of municipal administration[6] was highly appraised by Zoltán Magyary.

Professor Andor Csizmadia took a deep interest in social matters as well; one of his publications describes the tendencies of social policy inherent in the employment contracts of dualistic law.[7] His book *A szociális gondoskodás változásai Magyarországon* [Changes in social care in Hungary][8] published in 1977 is considered to be fundamental. It is made clear in this book that the first signs of social care appeared as early as the 19th century.

He wrote several studies on public service and on public administration qualifications; it may be noticed that their writer approached these issues with the confidence ensured by experience, practical knowledge and a historical and comparative aspect, and that he deemed the examination of the administrative staff of the dualistic administration indispensable. He also paid attention to the phenomenon of bureaucracy. His work *Bürokrácia és közigazgatási reformok Magyarhonban* [Bureaucracy and public administration reforms in Hungary. Collected documents],[9] a collection of sources and other documents, frequently used by members of the profession, was published in 1979. A major part of these documents, dug out of archives, files and neglected manuscripts by Andor Csizmadia, cover the generations of the dualistic era.

His work *A kormányzás egyes kérdései a felszabadulás előtt* [Some issues concerning government before the liberation in 1945][10] dealt with government. His work *A miniszteri felelősség kialakulása és fejlődése Magyarországon* [The development of ministerial responsibility in Hungary],[11] published in 1981 is also noticeable. These basic works are interwoven with the events of the dualistic era – quite naturally, as the bourgeois era in

---

[5] *A magyar állam és az egyházak jogi kapcsolatainak kialakulása és gyakorlata a Horthy-korszakban*, Budapest 1966, p. 442. *Rechtliche Beziehungen von Staat und Kirche in Ungarn vor 1944*, Budapest 1971, p. 296.

[6] *A városi közigazgatás egyszerűsítése* [The simplification of municipal administration] Budapest [1944], Statisztikai közlemények vol. 97, nr 1, p. 153.

[7] *Sozialpolitische Tendenzen in der Regelung der Arbeitsverhältnisse in Ungarn*, [in:] *Die Entwicklung des Zivilrechts in Mitteleuropa 1848–1944* [Socio-political trends in the regulation of labour relations in Hungary], [in:] The development of civil law in Central Europe. 1848–1944, Budapest 1970, pp. 347–369.

[8] *A szociális gondoskodás változásai Magyarországon* [Changes in social care in Hungary], Budapest 1977, p. 328.

[9] *Bürokrácia és közigazgatási reformok Magyarhonban. Dokumentumgyűjtemény* [Bureaucracy and public administration reforms in Hungary. Collected documents]. (Közreadja, válogatta, sajtó alá rendezte, a szemelvények bevezetését és jegyzeteit, valamint a bevezető tanulmányt írta Csizmadia Andor), Budapest 1979, p. 585.

[10] *A kormányzás egyes kérdései a felszabadulás előtt* [Some issues concerning government before the liberation in 1945], Budapest 1983, p. 366.

[11] *A miniszteri felelősség kialakulása és fejlődése Magyarországon* [The development of ministerial responsibility in Hungary], [in:] *A miniszteri és államtitkári felelősség* [The responsibility of ministers and under-secretaries of state], Budapest 1981, pp. 5–64.

1919–1944 emphasized legal continuity in the legal system and in the operation of state machinery.

The above works prepared his book which is regarded as his principal work by legal historians *A magyar közigazgatás fejlődése a XVIII. századtól a tanácsrendszer létrejöttéig* [The development of Hungarian public administration from the 18th century to the establishment of the council system in 1950],[12] which was received by reviewers with pleasure and appraisal. *Suffice* it is to quote Alajos Degré, the other outstanding legal historian, "An imposing and detailed synthesis of a branch of our legal history of the capitalist era has been accomplished ensuring a useful starting point for the researchers of details as well."[13] More than one-third of the book covers the dualistic era. This is the apex of the description of the public administration of the era of the Compromise in Csizmadia's works. The material disclosed is unbelievably rich, he processed documents which were hard to have access to and carefully analysed several hundreds of items found in archives. The attitudes of politicians get understandable and the concealed power-political world of the era gets evaluated.

The popular work *Történelmünk a jogalkotás tükrében, Sarkalatos honi törvényeinkből 1001–1949* [Hungarian history as reflected in law-making. Some fundamental Hungarian Acts, 1001–1949][14] published in 1966 together with Beér János is one of his books on the sources of law and on codification. This often used book has become an obligatory item of the high standard reference libraries of history and social sciences. It publishes the most important legal sources of dualistic legislation together with notes and commentaries. Besides the macro level, the professor was also interested in local legislation, which is shown by the all-inclusive analysis of the legislation of comitat Tolna during the whole bourgeois era including dualism.[15]

The administration of justice is analysed in his study entitled *Az esküdtbíróság Magyarországon a dualizmus korában* [Courts with a jury in Hungary in the dualistic era].[16] The establishment of juries was a civil demand. It was introduced in cases concerning the press in 1848 and was renewed in 1867. Juries for criminal cases were set up in the Hungarian court system at the end of the 19th century, but their operation was substantially restricted before the world war and they were soon totally abolished.

In his works he also dealt with human rights, family law, the law of village communities and the legal historical issues concerning the Crown. It should be noted that he also studied the modernisation of the structure and operation of forest, pasture and vine-growing communities in the dualistic era in *A falusi közösségek szervezete és működése*

---

[12] *A magyar közigazgatás fejlődése a XVIII. századtól a tanácsrendszer létrejöttéig* [The development of Hungarian public administration from the 18th century to the establishment of the council system in 1950], Budapest 1976, p. 560.

[13] Jogtudományi Közlöny, 1977, pp.173–174.

[14] *Történelmünk a jogalkotás tükrében. Sarkalatos honi törvényeinkből 1001–1949* [Hungarian history as reflected in law-making. Some fundamental Hungarian Acts, 1001–1949], Közreadja: Beér János és Csizmadia Andor, Budapest 1966, p. 745.

[15] *Jogszabályalkotás Tolna megyében* [Legislation in comitat Tolna], [in:] *Tanulmányok Tolna megye történetéről*, V. Szekszárd 1974, pp. 399–458.

[16] *Az esküdtbíróság Magyarországon a dualizmus korában* [Courts with a jury in Hungary in the dualistic era], [in:] *Jogtörténeti tanulmányok I.*, Budapest 1966, pp. 131–148.

Magyarországon 1848 és 1944 között [The structure and operation of village communities in Hungary between 1848 and 1944].[17] What he published about the above issues became timely and served as one of the basic materials for the new regulation in the period following his death in 1985.

Besides being a lecturer and a researcher, he made a substantial contribution to the development of modern teaching materials of Hungarian constitutional law. His efforts in this respect were crowned by the publication of a textbook on Hungarian constitutional law (1972).[18] This was considered to be the standard textbook for generations of law students. Csizmadia was the co-editor and also the co-author of cardinal parts of this textbook. A remarkable emphasis was placed on the study of dualism from a legal historical aspect. Professor Csizmadia wrote a fifty-page-long history of the state of that period. The picture presented by him is never purely static; he always explains the power-political background and the development and possible distortion of institutions. Thus, contrary to the purely descriptive method, the approach applied can be regarded as clearly dynamic-functional.

Besides the actual trends in science policy and the problems to be solved by the legal historians' profession, his previous experience gained in practice also confirmed his choice of subject. As a researcher he was diligent and well-organised, exploited time optimally, planned his work carefully, strived after historical information of a wide range, applied a critical approach towards sources, and then utilising research documentation, made the legal historical picture by sweeping strokes of the brush.

As a research organiser he guided the creation of draft studies and research programmes and was extremely active in the Hungarian Lawyers' Association and in the Scientific Committee on Legal History of the Section of Law of the Hungarian Academy of Sciences. His activity as an editor also speaks for itself as he edited or co-edited approximately two dozen books. The professor had a key role in gaining international acknowledgement of the achievements of Hungarian legal history, he attended and organised innumerable conferences and was admitted to several international associations of legal historians.

Volume 2 of the Studies on the history of law is of special importance to us as it was edited by the professor and published in 1968 with the sub-title *A dualizmus korának állam – és jogtörténeti kérdései* [Issues of the state and legal history of dualism].[19] The twenty-three studies written by authors of different countries may be regarded as a comprehensive work: jurisprudence, international comparison, the history of politics and thought, different branches of law and legal institutions all contribute to the accomplished picture. This book praises professor Csizmadia as the organiser of research into the dualistic era. A publication of a similar quality is *Die Freiheitsrechte und die Staatstheorien*

---

[17] *A falusi közösségek szervezete és működése Magyarországon 1848 és 1944 között* [The structure and operation of village communities in Hungary between 1848 and 1944], [in:] Bolla Ilona, Csizmadia Andor, Degré Alajos, Horváth Pál, Tanulmányok a falusi közösségekről [Studies on village communities]. A Pécsi Tudományegyetem tanszékének Kiadványai. 2. Pécs 1977, pp. 35–53.

[18] Csizmadia Andor, Kovács Kálmán, Asztalos László: *Magyar állam- és jogtörténet. Egyetemi tankönyv* [Hungarian state and legal history. University textbook], Csizmadia Andor (ed.), Budapest 1972, p. 706.

[19] *Jogtörténeti tanulmányok II. A dualizmus korának állam – és jogtörténeti kérdései* [Studies on the history of law II. Issues of the state and legal history of dualism] eds. Csizmadia Andor, Pecze Ferenc, Budapest 1968.

im Zeitalter des Dualismus [Civil rights and theories of state in the Austro-Hungarian Monarchy]. Papers of the 7th Hungarian-Czechoslovak Conference on the history of law. Pécs, September 23–25, 1965. Edited by Csizmadia Andor, Budapest 1966.[20]

Andor Csizmadia, who died in 1985, was one of the determinative characters of the science of Hungarian legal history during his half-century activity. His life achievement conveys to us remarkable results of research conducted into the dualistic era, too.

Prof. Andor Csizmadia Dr. Dr. h.c. and His Research
into the Legal History of Dualism

Summary

Professor Andor Csizmadia (1910–1985), doctor honoris causa of the Jagiellonian University in Krakow, was one of the most outstanding figures of Hungarian legal history in the second part of the 20th century. Following his career in public administration, he taught in Eger, at the Faculty of Law in Budapest, and then at the Department of Legal History of the Faculty of Law in Pécs from 1958 to 1980. He published more than three hundred books, studies and scientific articles. His main field of interest covered local governments, especially the legal history of municipalities, the relationship between State and Church, social administration and the history of public service, although he also dealt with the history of suffrage and legal higher education. He paid attention to describing legal traditions and took a deep interest in the prominent characters of constitutional history as well. A remarkable emphasis was placed on the era of dualism in his life-work. His publications of sources were voluminous. This is manifested in his main work *A magyar közigazgatás fejlődése a XVIII. századtól a tanácsrendszer létrejöttéig* [The development of Hungarian public administration from the 18th century to the establishment of the council system in 1950] and in his textbook. He edited books on the private law and human rights of the dualistic era. The achievements of Professor Csizmadia in the field of the legal history of dualism have proved to be of permanent value.

---

[20] Studia iuridica auctoritate Universitatis Pécs, publicata 48.

Krisztina Korsósné Delacasse

Gerichtsverfassung und Justizwesen in Ungarn um die Jahrhundertwende

Kurzer Überblick der tatsächlichen Verwirklichung der Trennung von Justiz und Verwaltung – richterliche Unabhängigkeit und Verwaltungsgerichtsbarkeit

Während der Annäherung der Konzeption der Ungaren und des Kaisers verkündete Franz Joseph am 20. Oktober 1860 das Oktoberdiplom, und demzufolge wurde eine Kommission laut der Kandidierung des *Iudex Curiae*, also des Landesrichters zusammengerufen. Die Kommission, die unter dem Vorsitz des Landesrichters zusammensaß, und die man in der Rechtshistorik Judexkurialkonferenz nennt, verabschiedete nach den Verhandlungen die so genannte Judexkurialbeschlüsse, die provisorische Gerichtsnormen beinhaltete, die im Bereich der Gerichtsverfassung außer des Patrimonialgerichts eigentlich die früheren, vor 1848 existierten Gerichtsforen retablierte. Dieses System entsprach aber den neuen, modernen Ansprüchen ganz und gar nicht. Es wurde die Modernisierung des ganzen Gerichtswesens nötig, eine solche Aufbau der Justiz, die entsprechend der liberalen Staatsgedanken in das System der Montesquieuschen Gewaltentrennung eingepasst werden konnte. Die Konkretisierung der staatsorganisatorischen Vorstellungen von 1848 und der in den so genannten Aprilgesetzen deklarierten Institutionen wurde endlich auch unter friedlichen und ruhigen Umständen ab 1867 möglich.

Nach dem Ausgleich war in Ungarn die erste Frage auf dieser Ebene der Ausbau der selbständigen richterlichen Organisation. Den ersten Schritt in diese Richtung führte der GA 1868:LIV., der die bürgerliche Gerichtsordnung regelte. Die meritorische Neuerung dieses Gesetzes war die organisatorische Trennung der Zentralen oberen Gerichte: der königlichen Tafel, des Wechselobergerichtes und der Septemviraltafel. Demnach wurde als „Kurie" nur die letztere genannt, die als oberstes Gericht des Staates vom nächsten Jahr an in zwei Klassen arbeitete: Kassationshof und Oberster Gerichtshof. Den bürgerlichen Anforderungen war die Reform gewachsen, dass die Mitgliederzahl der Gerichtssenate in Zivilsachen bei den erstinstanzlichen Gerichten in drei und bei den königlichen Tafeln in fünf bestimmt wurde; die Verwirklichung der Kollegialgerichtsbarkeit schon an niedrigen Instanzen war nicht nur nach der Axiome *plures oculi, plura vident* sondern auch als beste „Rezeptur" gegen das richterlichen Willkür wichtiges Erfordernis in der zeitgenössischen Literatur.[1] 1869 schieden die feudalen Beisitzer aus.

Die Prinzipien der neuen Gerichtsorganisation wurden jedoch erst durch das Gesetz 1869:IV. über die Ausübung der richterlichen Macht niedergelegt. In dieser Norm folgte man fast Wort für Wort den entsprechenden Teilen der belgischen Verfassung von 1830.[2] Durch dieses Gesetz wurde also die Trennung der Verwaltung und der Justiz[3] und nicht zuletzt die Unabhängigkeit der Richter festgestellt. Letztere bedeutete vor allem die Maxime, dass der Richter ausschließlich zu den Gesetzen und zu den gesetzkräftigen Gewohnheiten (d.h. Gewohnheitsrecht) und zu den aufgrund von Gesetzen entstandenen und verkündeten Verordnungen gebunden ist. Die Formulierung dieses Paragraphen war nicht ohne Probleme, die dem Partikularismus des früheren traditionellen Rechts[4], und dessen vielfältigen Rechtsquellen zu danken war.[5] In der früheren Literatur war zwar auch die Ansicht vertreten, dass die Unabhängigkeit der Richter sich in die tausendjährige Verfassung eingebettet schon vor Jahrhunderten verwirklicht worden war, aber die Unhaltbarkeit dieser Auffassung wurde durch die rechtshistorischen Kritik bewiesen.[6] Wichtig ist aber hinzufügen, dass die Tatsache, dass man den Begriff der Unabhängigkeit nicht benutzt hatte, schließt das Bestehen des Wesens selbst nicht aus. Wie Degré feststellte: „der Begriff der richterlichen Unabhängigkeit ändert sich nicht, nur die Institutionen, die sie sichern".[7]

Welche waren also die neuen Bestimmungen, die zum Erreichen dieser Zielsetzung führten? Das Gesetz band die Ernennung zum Richter an Befähigungsnachweis, schrieb die Anforderungen des Richterlichen Amtes und die Grundsätze der Inkompatibilität vor. Im Parlament war die Ernennung der Richter heftig diskutiert, die Opposition hätte

---

[1] Máthé Gábor, *A bírói hatalom gyakorlásáról szóló 1869:4. tc. létrejötte és jelentősége a dualizmus jogrendszerében* [Die Entstehung und Bedeutung des GA 1869:4. im Rechtssystem des Dualismus], [in:] Mezey Barna (Hg.), *Jogtörténeti értekezések 31. Ünnepi tanulmányok Kovács Kálmán egyetemi tanár emlékére Gondolat Kiadó*, Budapest 2005, S. 37–70.

[2] Bónis György, Degré Alajos, Varga Endre, *A magyar bírósági szervezet és perjog története* [Die Geschichte der ungarischen Rechtspflege und des Prozessrechts] Zalaegerszeg 1996, S. 215.

[3] Es wird aber darauf hingedeutet, dass auch dieses Gesetz nicht in allen Punkten völlig konsequent war: die Gerichte hatten auch typische verwalterische Aufgaben (z.B. die Grundbuchführung), und die Beurteilung von bestimmten Bagatellstrafsachen blieb weiterhin in der Kompetenz der Verwaltungsbehörden.
Stipta István, *A magyar bírósági rendszer története* [Die Geschichte der ungarischen Gerichtsorganisation] Multiplex Media, Debrecen University Press, Debrecen 1997, S. 122; Máthé Gábor, *Die Problematik der Gewaltentrennung*, Gondolat Verlag, Budapest 2004, S. 127.

[4] In der Geschichte des ungarischen Rechts bedeutete 1848 eine Epochengrenze. Das Recht der vorherigen Periode kann – mit neueren, von Gábor Béli konstruierten Bezeichnung – als traditionelles Recht anzusehen, da dieses Begriff am meisten geeignet ist, diejenige Eigentümlichkeit des alten ungarischen Rechts zum Ausdruck zu bringen, dass dessen fundamentale Institutionen sich durch die Übermittlung des Gewohnheitsrecht entwickelten und weiterlebten, und manche Prinzipien sich sogar von der Zeit der Gentilordnung forterbten.
Béli Gábor, *Magyar jogtörténet. A tradicionális jog* [Ungarische Rechtsgeschichte. Das traditionelles Recht] Dialóg Campus Kiadó, Budapest–Pécs 2000, S. 20.

[5] Máthé (Anm. 1), S. 57–58.

[6] Degré Alajos, *Adatok a magyar bírói függetlenség múltjához* [Angaben zur Vergangenheit der ungarischen richterlichen Unabhängigkeit], [in:] Degré Alajos, *Válogatott jogtörténeti tanulmányok* [Ausgewählte rechtshistorische Studien] (Hg. Mezey Barna), S. 87.

[7] Degré (Anm. 6), S. 88.

am liebsten die Wahl als Prinzip betrachten.[8] Zusammenfassend wollte man die richterliche Unabhängigkeit im Gesetz mit den folgenden Maßnahmen noch mehr sichern und unterzeichnen[9]:
- die Richter bekommen ihren Gehalt aus der Staatskasse, und der Gehalt darf nicht reduziert werden. Die Richter müssen aber den Parteien ohne besondere Belohnung Recht sprechen. Es bezieht sich natürlich nicht auf die gesetzlich festgestellten Gerichtsgebühren.
- Der gesetzmäßig ernannte Richter kann aus seinem Amt nicht entfernt werden, es sei denn es um einen im Gesetz bestimmten Grund geht.
- Den Richter darf man – außer den im Gesetz aufgelisteten Gründen – nur aus eigenem Willen von seinem Sitz nach einen anderen versetzen oder auch befördert werden.
- Die Versetzung in den Ruhestand kann nur im Fall von Unfähigkeit der Pflichterfüllung wegen Alters (70 Jahre), geistiges oder körperliches Fehlers erfolgen.
- Abschaffung von Gesetzmäßig aufgestelltem Gericht, Errichten neuer Gerichte, Änderung der Zuständigkeit, der Gerichtskreise, und der Anzahl der Richter außer dem Gesetzgebungswege sind untersagt.

Die königlichen Gerichtstafeln und die Kurie blieben zunähst unberührt, aber die Neuorganisation der erstinstanzlicher Gerichte auf Grund der in dem vorher genannten Gesetz festgelegten Grundsätze wurde 1871 durch weiteren zwei Gesetze verwirklicht. (GA 1871:XXXI. und GA 1871:XXXII.). Nach der neuen Ordnung war das erstinstanzliche Gericht von allgemeiner Zuständigkeit der königliche Gerichtshof. In den – früher zum Stuhlrichter, der Richter und Verwaltungsbeamte in einem war, gehörigen – kleineren Zivil- und Strafsachen, die das Gesetz ausdrücklich in die Sphäre der Kreisgerichte zuwies, verfuhren diese.

Die Einführung einer Verwaltungsgerichtsbarkeit war derzeit noch nicht geplant. (Wenn man die Lage mit der in Österreich vergleichen will, gab es zu dieser Zeit auch im anderen Teil der Monarchie kein solches Gericht, das die Überprüfung der rechtswidrigen Entscheidungen von Verwaltungsbehörden gegenüber Staatsbürger zur Aufgabe hatte. Das im Jahr 1869 in Österreich Aufgestellte Reichsgericht wurde nur im Fall der Verletzung der in der Verfassung deklarierten Grundrechte – vor allem politischer Rechte – der Staatsbürger angerufen, und der Verwaltungsgerichtshof wurde schließlich erst 1876 geschaffen, obwohl es einen getrennten Staatsgerichtshof schon seit 1867 auch gab, dem die gerichtliche Ahndung von Verfassungs- und Gesetzesverletzungen der Minister oblag.[10])

Mit einem Gesetz – ebenfalls aus dem Jahr 1871 (GA XXXIII.) wurde die bisher in Ungarn in dieser Form nicht existierende Staatsanwaltschaft, als selbständige Organisation der öffentlichen Anklage, ins Leben gerufen. Die Einteilung der Staatsanwaltschaft entsprach der der Gerichte, also neben der königlichen Kurie stand der „Kronen(staats)

---

[8] Die Gegner des Ernennungssystems waren vor allem die Komitate, die auch noch nach dem Inkrafttreten des Gesetzes Petitionen zum Abgeordnetenhaus sendeten. Máthé Gábor, *A magyar burzsoá igazságszolgáltatási szervezet kialakulása (1867–1875)* [Die Ausbildung der ungarischen bürgerlichen Gerichtsorganisation 1867–1875] Akadémiai Kiadó, Budapest 1982, S. 50–52.

[9] Máthé (Anm. 8), S. 42.

[10] Brauneder Wilhelm, Lachmayer Friedrich, *Österreichische Verfassungsgeschichte*, Manz Verlag, Wien 1987, S. 160–161.

anwalt" (ca. Generalstaatsanwalt), diese Position blieb aber bis zum Ende des Jahrhunderts unbesetzt, erst nach dem Inkrafttreten der neuen Strafprozessordnung aus dem Jahre 1896. Neben die Gerichtstafeln stellte man königlichen Oberstaatsanwaltschaften, neben die königlichen Gerichtshöfe königliche Staatsanwaltschaften auf. In den Bezirken wurden keine Staatsanwaltschaften organisiert, sondern Substitutus-Saatsanwälte angestellt. Wichtig ist hier, dass nach langer parlamentarischer Diskussion die Staatsanwaltschaft der Regierung, bzw. dem Justizminister untergeordnet wurde. Die Oberstaatsanwaltschaften waren unmittelbar dem Minister unterstellt und standen unter seiner Leitung. Der Kronenanwalt hatte keine Aufsichts- und Weisungsrechte über die Staatsanwaltschaft.[11]

Wenn man über Justizwesen spricht, müssen auch die weiteren wichtigen Teilnehmer der Rechtsanwendung erwähnt werden, die Rechtsanwälte und die Notare. In den Jahren 1874 bzw. 1875 wurden diesen Instituten neu geregelt, sogar neu aufgestellt. Die Rechtsanwälte hatten bisher eigentlich keine Organisation, und auch keine gesetzliche Regelung. Die königliche Notare nahmen die Aufgaben der bisherigen so genannten „glaubwürdigen Orten" über, also die öffentliche Glaubwürdigkeit bekam dadurch statt kirchlicher Organe eine weltliche Charakter. Die Ausübung beider genannten juristischen Berufe war durch die Mitgliedschaft in den Kanzleien möglich.

So sah kurz gefasst das System aus, die um die Jahrhundertwende umgestaltet wurde.

Die Umorganisierung der Obergerichte wurde schrittweise geschaffen. Nach der schon erwähnten Änderung der Mitglieder[12] geschah die wichtigste Umformung im Jahre 1881 (GA 1881:LIX.). Der Kassationshof wurde abgeschafft und die Kurie wurde demzufolge zu einem einheitlichen Obersten Gerichtshof organisiert. Das GA 1890:XXV. dezentralisierte die königliche Gerichtstafeln und statt der bisherigen zwei richtete insgesamt elf Gerichtstafeln ein.[13]

Die Geschworenengerichte waren bis zum Ende des XIX. Jahrhunderts nur neben einigen Gerichten zum Verfahren in Presseprozessen berufen und nur durch Verordnung geregelt. Mit dem Gesetzartikel XXXIII. vom Jahre 1897 etablierte man fast neben alle Gerichte Geschworenenbänke, die in erster Linie in den schweren Strafsachen urteilten, und schon eine regelmäßige Tätigkeit ausübten.[14]

In dem im Untertitel erwähnten Zusammenhang sind aber vor allem bestimmte außerordentliche Gerichte erwähnenswert, da diese – meiner Meinung nach – einen engeren Zusammenhang zu den Staatsgedanken und zum Verfassungsrecht hatten.[15]

---

[11] Máthé (Anm. 8), pS. 155–160. Über die parlamentarische Debatte: Delacasse Krisztina, *A modern vádképviseleti rendszer meghonosítása Magyarországon* [Die Einführung des modernen Anklagevertretungssystems in Ungarn], [in:] Jogtudományi Közlöny 1997/10, S. 424–432.

[12] Entfernen der feudalen Beisitzer der Gerichte.

[13] Die Umorganisierung wird detailliert dargestellt: Antal Tamás, *Törvénykezési reformok Magyarországon 1890–1900* [Gerichtsreforme in Ungarn 1890–1900] Szeged 2006.

[14] Über die Geschworenengerichte während der Dualismus Csizmadia Andor, *Az esküdtbíróság Magyarországon a dualizmus korában* [Das Geschworenengericht in Ungarn in der Zeit des Dualismus], [in:] *Jogtörténeti Tanulmányok I*, Budapest 1966, S. 131–148; Antal (Anm. 12).

[15] Weitere außerordentliche Gerichte der Epoche, die jedoch nicht eng zu diesem Thema gehören, waren das Patentamt, das 1895 auch in gerichtlicher Form, später auch mit dem Namen Patentgericht organisiert wurde, und das Hofmarschallgericht. Die Aufstellung dieses letzten außerordentlichen Gerichts (1909), das in

Ein sehr wichtiger Schritt auf dem Weg der Verwirklichung der Gewaltentrennung war das Aufstellen des Verwaltungsgerichtshofes (GA 1896:XXVI.). Dadurch entstand die Möglichkeit der Staatsbürger, gegen die Missbräuche der Verwaltungsbehörden sich zum unabhängigen Forum, also zum Gericht, und zwar zum speziellen Gericht zuzuwenden.[16] Die Voraussetzungen eines Rechtsstaates benötigten aber auch ein selbstständiges und unabhängiges Forum, das in den Zuständigkeitsstreiten unter Gerichte und Verwaltungsbehörden richtete, aber das konnte man in Ungarn erst nach der Jahrhundertwende realisieren.

Der Gedanke solcher Gerichte ist ziemlich früh aufgetaucht. Schon während der Debatte des Gesetzartikels 1869:IV. beantragte ein Abgeordneter der parlamentarischen Opposition erfolglos, dass ein Bürger, der sich in seinen Rechten durch einen Verwaltungsbeschluss verletzt fühlt, den richterlichen Weg in Anspruch nehmen könne, und zwar in der Form des normalen Gerichtsverfahrens vor dem allgemein zuständigen Richter.[17] Da es aber zu weit führen würde, muss man hier auf die detaillierte Vorführung aller früheren Diskussionen verzichten. Ich beschränke mich also nur auf die unmittelbaren Vorereignisse des obgenannten Gesetzes. Das schon erwähnte bedeutende Gesetz über die richterliche Macht verbarg aber auch eine Schranke in sich, worauf die Gegner der Verwaltungsgerichtsbarkeit beziehen konnten. Der Paragraph 1. dieses Gesetzes lautete nämlich so, dass die Verwaltungs- und Justizbehörden in die Kompetenz von einander nicht eingreifen dürfen. Demzufolge wurde die Ausdehnung der Tätigkeit der ordentlichen richterlichen Foren auf streitige administrative Angelegenheiten ausgeschlossen. Es gab aber auch eigenartige Widersprüche, weil einzelne spätere Gesetze den Angriff auf Verwaltungsbeschlüsse von dem ordentlichen Gericht ermöglichten.[18]

Als Problem in der Regelung dieses Gebiets muss auch erwähnt werden, dass in den ersten Jahren des Dualismus eher die Seite der Justizgewalt untersucht war. Zahlreiche Studien und Vorlagen beschäftigten sich mit dem Ausbau der selbständigen richterlichen Organisation, mit der Problemen der Wahl oder Ernennung der Richter, mit der Unabhängigkeit dieser, aber nach der Feststellung des ausgezeichneten ungarischen Forschers dieses Themas – Gábor Máthé – ist auffallend, dass die allgemeinen theoretischen Fragen der neuen Justizorganisation nicht behandelt wurden und besonders die Klärung des Verhältnisses zur Verwaltung außer Acht gelassen wurde.[19] Auch der zeitgenössische Károly Csemegi wies darauf hin, dass die primitive Zustand der Verwaltungsapparat und die damit zusammenhängende „theoretische Begründung" zur Bestimmung der einzelnen Machtbereiche der Gerichte und der Verwaltung nicht als Grundlage dienen könnten.[20] Grundsätzliche Frage war also, dass die Justizorganisation nur neben einem entwickelten Verwaltungssystem mit klar umrissenen Kompetenzen und Organisationen in Gleichgewicht wirken kann. In den Jahren 1870 und 1871 entstanden die zwei Grundgesetze der zeitgemäßen bürgerlichen Verwaltung. In dieser öffentlich-rechtlichen Kon-

---

der Zivilsachen der königlichen Familie und in denen der zum Hof gehörigen Personen verfuhr, unterzeichnete eher den monarchischen Charakter des Staates. Bónis, Degré, Varga (Anm. 2), S. 223.

[16] *Idem* (Anm. 2), S. 221.

[17] Máthé (Anm. 3), S. 53.

[18] Stipta (Anm. 3), S. 140.

[19] Máthé (Anm. 3), S. 46.

[20] *Idem* (Anm. 3), S. 47.

struktion, wo die Regierung eine bedeutende Rolle gegenüber der Munizipien spielte, wäre die Schaffung eines Gerichts, das gegen die rechtswidrigen Maßnahmen und gegen die Versäumnisse der verfahrenden Behörden Schutz bietet, besonders wichtig. In den Jahren des früheren Dualismus geschah nur eine wichtige Fortschritt auf dem Gebiet des öffentlich-rechtlichen Schutzes: der GA 1874:XXXIII. über das Wahlrecht und Wahlverfahren ermöglichte im Fall der Verletzung des Wahlrechts die Appellation zur Kurie.

Obwohl es sowohl nach der herrschenden wissenschaftlichen Auffassung als auch nach den anspruchsvollen öffentlichen politischen Meinungen ratsam war, beschäftigte sich die Regierung lange nicht ernst mit der Problematik.[21] Erst in den '80-en Jahren hat sich die ungarische Politik endlich entschlossen, die Institution einer allgemeinen Verwaltungsgerichtsbarkeit zu schaffen. Nämlich die Fachberatung des Innenministeriums, die zur Besprechung der Verwaltungsreformen zusammentrat, sprach sowohl die Nötigkeit als auch das ernste Willen der Regierung zur Durchführung dieser Änderungen aus.[22] Der Weg zur endgültigen Lösung der Problematik war aber noch lang.

Die erste und wichtigste Frage war, ob die die administrative Beschlüsse überprüfende Körperschaft von den ordentlichen Gerichten getrennt oder in deren Organisation verbleibend wirken sollte. Auch die die Sitzungen des Reichstags im Jahre 1881 eröffnende Thronrede des Königs beinhaltete die Aufgabe, die Aufstellung der Verwaltungsgerichte in je kürzerer Zeit zu bewerkstelligen. Die Regierung fertigte noch in diesem Jahr zwei Pläne an. Der erste, der ein aus Verwaltungsbeamten, Richtern und Laien bestandenes Fachgericht konzipierte, stieß auf harten Widerstand der öffentlichen Meinung. Der andere Entwurf organisierte ein unabhängiges Gericht in Finanzangelegenheiten.[23] Solche Gerichtsforen, die so genannte Gefällsgerichte, die in Fällen von Steuer- und Finanzbeschwerden wirkten, wurden schon 1867 aufgestellt und im nächsten Jahr als Finanzgerichte umgeformt, aber sie könnten ihre Tätigkeit nur einigen Jahren lang entfalten, weil sie 1872 bzw. 1873 abgeschafft wurden.[24]

Auch die 1882 zusammengerufene Ungarische Juristenversammlung nahm das Problem auf ihre Tagesordnung. Die obigen zwei verschiedenen Meinungen kamen auch hier vor. Der eine Antrag (Győző Concha) sah vor, dass mit der Verwaltungsrechtsprechung die ordentlichen Gerichte befasst werden sollten und die Gerichte sollten vor allem die Gesetzmäßigkeit und „den Schutz der aus öffentlichen Verhältnissen stammenden privaten Rechte" vor Augen halten.[25] Der andere Standpunkt, der von der Mehrheit akzeptiert wurde, sah die Verwaltungsgerichtsbarkeit als eine *sui generis* Tätigkeit, zu deren Erfüllung man eine spezifische Organisation braucht.

Endlich gebar das Gesetz über die Finanzverwaltungsgerichtsbarkeit 1883[26] und rief ein einziges Forum ins Leben, die nur beschränkte Kompetenz hatte. In seinen Wir-

---

[21] Stipta István, *Országgyűlési vita a pénzügyi közigazgatási bíróságról 1883-ban* [Parlamentarische Debatte über die Finanzverwaltunggerichtsbarkeit 1883], [in:] Mezey Barna, Révész T. Mihály (Hg.), *Ünnepi tanulmányok Máthé Gábor 65. születésnapja tiszteletére* [Festschrift zum 65. Geburtstag von Gábor Máthé], Gondolat Kiadó, Budapest 2006, S. 518–546.

[22] Stipta István, *Die Verikale Gewaltentrennung*, Gondolat Verlag, Budapest 2005, S. 170.

[23] *Idem* (Anm. 3), S. 141.

[24] Bónis, Degré, Varga (Anm. 2), S. 222.

[25] Stipta (Anm. 22), S. 171.

[26] Mit der parlamentarischen Debatte beschäftigt sich detailliert: Stipta (Anm. 21).

kungskreis gerieten nur solche Angelegenheiten, in denen die Behörden – ob sie Selbstverwaltungs- oder staatliche Organe seien – in Steuer- und Gebührsachen Entscheidung getroffen hatten. In diesen Fragen entschied das Finanzgerichtshof als erst- und letztinstanzliches Forum in schriftlichem Verfahren, gegebenenfalls auch mit reformatorischer Auswirkung. Das Gericht bestand einerseits aus Fachleuten aus der Verwaltung, die mit den nötigen theoretischen und praktischen Qualifikation verfügten, andererseits aus früheren Richtern. Nach einigen Jahren stellte sich aber heraus, dass das einstufige Gericht die Erledigung der vielen Verfahren nur schwer leisten konnte, deshalb wurde schon 1889 selbst vom Präsident des Finanzgerichtshofes (Pál Madarassy) der Entwurf über die Aufstellung weiteren erstinstanzlichen Finanzgerichte eingereicht.[27]

Die Frage des allgemeinen Verwaltungsgerichts war aber noch immer nicht gelöst. Das Problem tauchte auch als Zusammenstoß zwischen Interessen der Regierung und der Munizipien, vor allem der Komitaten auf, die (die letztere) unter anderen das Aufsichtsrecht des Ministeriums kritisierten und im Abgeordnetenhaus wurde deshalb immer wieder um ein von der Regierung unabhängiges zentrales Forum (Gericht) mit Verwaltungskompetenz gebeten, das nicht nur auf den Schutz der Rechte der Bürger, sondern auch den Schutz der Selbstverwaltungsrechte gewährleisten könne. Den Grund zur „Wideraufbrennen" des Themas waren die Gesetzesentwürfe über die lokalen Verwaltungen 1886 (GA XXI., XXII.).[28] Auf eine solche Rechtsnorm, die ein Rechtsmittel gegen die Verordnungen des Ministers, die die Befugnis der Munizipien verletzten ermöglichte, musste man in Ungarn bis 1907 warten.[29]

Die letzte Vorstufe vor der Entstehung des Verwaltungsgerichtshofes war der GA 1891:XXXIII., die die Verallgemeinerung der administrativen Justiz vorsah und die Regierung verpflichtete, mit den Entwürfen über die Verwaltung zusammen auch einen Gesetzesentwurf über die Verwaltungsgerichtsbarkeit einzureichen.

Der damalige Innenminister (Károly Hieronymi) brachte seinen Vorschlag am 28. Oktober 1893 in das Abgeordnetenhaus ein. Er empfahl darin ein System von zweistufigen besonderen Fachgerichten, weil die Regierung die ordentlichen Gerichte nicht mit Verwaltungsverfahren belasten wollte. Die Meinung des Ministeriums war, dass es zwischen Zivil- und Verwaltungsangelegenheiten wesentlichen Unterschied gäbe. Nach langen Diskussionen und aus den für unsere öffentlich-rechtlichen Gesetzgebung immer charakteristischen Kompromissen entstand der GA 1896:XXVI. über die ungarische Verwaltungsgerichtsbarkeit.[30]

Der Verwaltungsgerichtshof wurde als zentrales Fachgericht organisiert, der außer dem System der ordentlichen Gerichte stand und dessen Präsident mit dem der Kurie in gleichem Rang stand. Er arbeitete in zwei Klassen: Allgemeine Verwaltung und Finanz. Mit der Aufstellung dieses Institutes wurde die bisherige Finanzgerichtshof eingestellt.

Der Entscheidung über die Befugnisse des Gerichts gingen lange Diskussionen voraus, endlich entschied sich der Gesetzgeber für die Taxation. Die Fälle also, in denen gegen die

---

[27] Stipta (Anm. 22), S. 173.

[28] *Idem* (Anm. 22), S. 173. bzw. S. 238–239, Máthé (Anm. 3).

[29] GA LX. 1907., Stipta (Anm. 3), S. 151.

[30] Stipta (Anm. 22), S. 178.

Beschlüsse der Verwaltungsbehörden der richterliche Weg offen war, wurden im Gesetz aufgelistet. Spätere Gesetze dehnten diesen Kreis auf weitere Angelegenheiten aus.[31]

Das letzte Ergebnis des demokratischen Rechtsstaates in dieser Epoche war das Zustande bringen des so genannten Kompetenzgerichtes, das in den Zuständigkeitsstreiten unter Gerichte und Verwaltungsbehörden richtete.[32] Obwohl die Frage der Aufstellung eines „Staatsgerichthofes", der z.B. in Kompetenzkollisionen zwischen Verwaltungsorganen, oder nach einem anderen Antrag auch in den Zuständigkeitszusammenstößen von Gerichte und Verwaltungsorgane zu entscheiden gehabt hätte, schon 1848 zur Tageslicht gekommen und nach dem Ausgleich im Abgeordnetenhaus immer wieder aufgeworfen war, erhielt dieser Vorschlag wie auch derjenige, der mit dieser Aufgabe den Kassationshof betrauen wollte, nicht das Einverstanden der Mehrheit.[33] Später – im Sinne der § 25. des GA 1869:IV. – war mit dieser Aufgabe provisorisch die Regierung befugt. Spätere Vorschriften unterzeichneten diesen Wirkungskreis des Ministerrats dadurch, dass sie dieses Organ mit der Entscheidung in weiteren Fällen befugten. Dass jedoch man diese nicht für die beste Lösung gehalten hat, zeigt auch ein Satz vom GA 1883:XLIII., die aussprach, dass diese Regelung nur solange in Kraft bliebe, bis ein Staatsrat, oder ein geeignetes höchstes Forum zur Entscheidung der Befugnis- und Kompetenzkollisionen ins Leben gerufen wird. Auch das Gesetz über die Verwaltungsgerichtsbarkeit beinhaltete eine ähnliche Vorschrift.[34] 1907 geschah es in der Form eines speziellen Gerichts, und dadurch wurde auch dieser alte verfassungsrechtliche Anspruch endlich zufrieden gestellt.

Zusammenfassend ist zu bemerken, dass die erste Periode des Dualismus auf dem Gebiet der Justiz – und parallel dazu auch in der Verwaltung – eher die Phase der Gründung eines modernen Systems war, die nur durch Kompromisse verwirklicht worden konnte. Die Geltendmachung der „rechtsstaatlichen Konstruktion" war kein einfacher Weg, es wurde vor allem von der Seite der Munizipien erschwert, die die Durchführung der Pläne der liberalen Politik in der Interesse ihrer „historischen Rechte" verhindern versuchten.[35] Dem Niederlegen der organisatorischen Grundlagen der neuen, den bürgerlichen Prinzipien entsprechenden Gerichtsverfassung, und dem allgemeinen Justizreform in den Jahren 1867–1875 folgte später – schon nach praktischen Erfahrungen – die Umformung und Differenzierung der Institute. Diese Feststellung klängt mit der Auffassung von István Kajtár zusammen, nach der sich auch die Epoche des Dualismus mit „Modernisationswellen" beschreiben lässt, von denen die erste Welle nach 1867, die zweite um die Jahrhundertwende anberaumt werden kann.[36] Empirische und theoretische Erwägungen und oft heftige politische-wissenschaftliche Diskussionen ebenfalls führten also zu den neuen Lösungen, die die weitere Vertiefung der rechtsstaatlichen Garantien

---

[31] *Idem* (Anm. 3), S. 150.

[32] GA 1907.LXI. Das Gericht entschied in den folgenden Kompetenzkollisionen: zwischen Gerichten und Verwaltungsorganen, zwischen dem Verwaltungsgerichtshof und den ordentlichen Gerichten, und zwischen dem Verwaltungsgerichtshof und Verwaltungsorganen.

[33] Stipta (Anm. 3), S. 137; Máthé (Anm. 3), S. 53.

[34] Stipta (Anm. 3), S. 152.

[35] Máthé (Anm. 3), S. 63, S. 93.

[36] Kajtár István, *A XIX. századi modern magyar állam – és jogrendszer alapjai. Európa – haladás – Magyarország* [Die Grundlagen des modernen ungarischen Staats- und Rechtssystems im 19. Jahrhundert. Europa – Fortschritt – Ungarn] Dialóg Campus Kiadó, Budapest–Pécs 2003, S. 103–105.

dienen konnten, und die als hochwertige Produkte der heimischen Rechtssetzung schon zur europäischen vordersten Linie gerechnet werden müssen.[37]

The Structure of the Courts and the Administration of Justice in Hungary at the Turn of the Century

Summary

The article emphasizes the extent to which the first period of Austro-Hungarian dualism was responsible for laying foundations for the modern system of the judiciary and the administration. In this respect the effects were reached through compromise. The arrival at the *Rechtsstaat* concept was not a simple thing since its effectiveness was impeded by the self-governmental municipal structures which tended toward preserving their *historical rights*. They therefore consequently provided obstacles for the plans of liberal politicians. However, the consolidation of the organizational foundations of the *Rechtsstaat* also in the area of the judiciary, was responsible for the modification and diversity of the Hungarian judicature, the reforms of 1867–1875 being of particular significance in this respect. This observation corresponds to what István Kajtar has pronounced when he emphasized that the period of dualism may be described as the *waves of modernization*, the first wave directly following 1867 while the second falling on the turn of the 20th century. At that time the empirical observation and theoretical analysis, accompanied by sharp political discussion in the world of learning, led to the new solutions. The latter allowed for the deepening of the guarantees offerred by the State. These solutions also merged with the Europe-wide tendency in the development of the judiciary.

---

[37] *Idem* (Anm. 36), S. 104.

Grzegorz M. Kowalski

Constitutional Liberty in the Area of Emigration in Austria (1867–1918). The Activities of the Emigration Agencies in Galicia and Lodomeria

1. Freedom of Emigration in Austria during Constitutional Period. Legal Bases

The legal system which was in force during the constitutional period in Austria guaranteed a wide range of rights and liberties to a man and a citizen, including the freedom of emigration. The fundamental Act of 21st December, 1867 *on general rights of a citizen*[1] in its regulation (article 4, sentences 3 and 4) constituted that, on the part of the state, the freedom of emigration is solely limited by a military service duty and the emigration fees may be charged exclusively on the basis of the principle of reciprocity.[2] Hence, the previously binding regulation, namely *the patent on emigration* of 1832,[3] was repealed; it differentiated between *legal*, i.e. permitted emigration (which in practice was limited due to a series of difficult conditions to be fulfilled), and *unentitled*, i.e. illegal. However, according to the doctrine, due to the lack of an Act regulating emigration issues, some regulations of the Patent of 1832 remained binding even after the constitution had come into force. These were the norms in no contradiction to the constitution itself, including but not limited to the regulation containing a legal definition of an emigrant or the regulations referring to the loss of Austrian citizenship as a result of emigration. These highly complex issues were perceived as disputable in jurisprudence.

However, there was no doubt that after the December Constitution entering into force there existed no formal limitations towards emigration except for the military duty.

---

[1] *Staatsgrundgesetz von 21. December 1867, über die allgemeinen Rechte der Staatsbürger für die im Reichsrathe vertretenen Königreiche und Länder*, Reichs-Gesetz-Blatt für das Kaiserthum Oesterreich Nr 142 (further quoted as: R.G.Bl.). More details on legal regulation of emigration in Austria may be found [in:] G.M. Kowalski, *Prawna regulacja wychodźstwa na ziemiach polskich pod panowaniem austriackim w latach 1832–1914*, "Czasopismo Prawno-Historyczne", t. LIV, 2002, z. 1, pp. 171–191; idem, *Przestępstwa emigracyjne w Galicji 1897–1918. Z badań nad dziejami polskiego wychodźstwa*, Kraków 2003, pp. 29–42.

[2] *Die Freiheit der Auswanderung ist von Staatswegen nur durch die Wehrpflicht beschränkt. Abfahrtsgelder dürfen nur in Anwendung der Reciprocität erhoben werden.*

[3] *Auswanderungs-Patent*, Provinzial-Gesetzsammlung des Königreichs Galizien und Lodomerien Nr 68, Lemberg 1834.

Therefore illegal emigration of recruits was regulated by the laws on military service.[4] Leaving the country for the purpose of evading military service was mainly subject to sanctions such as an arrest or a fine.

Despite the lack of an appropriate legal act regulating comprehensively the issue of emigration, the authorities did not infringe the freedom of emigration, which was guaranteed by the Constitution. Their attitude towards the whole problem of emigration, which was based on the Constitution of 1867, did not change even when envisaging tense political situation one day before the outbreak of the First World War. Moreover, rumours about limitation of freedom to emigrate were considered such a serious problem, that in spring of 1914 the Lieutenancy decided to make an announcement to the citizens, which was to be printed in official journals, newspapers as well as stuck on billposts.[5] It confirmed in particular that the freedom of emigration, which was guaranteed by the Constitution, shall in no way be affected:

> Recently the public opinion has numerously expressed the view that the government via the issuance of new police regulations, regardless of the right to freely emigrate guaranteed by fundamental acts and limited only by the military service obligation, has generally forbade emigration to persons aged between 17. and 36. (...) It must be pointed out that authoritative circles are far from issuing a ban on emigration for certain age groups and introducing the overall temporary limitation on emigration, which appears to be a necessity for some regions due to an adverse economical situation.

The announcement also informed about the required norms for documents essential to cross the border by persons liable to military service.

Regarding other issues associated with the freedom to emigrate in Austria, some attention should be paid to documents essential to cross the border and leave the country. In the period of constitutional monarchy in Austria the obligation of carrying a passport was non-existent. The ultimate repeal of obligatory passport control was carried out via the Emperor's decree of 6th November, 1865.[6] The person crossing the border was liable to passport control exclusively in particular cases, e.g. in case there existed a well-grounded suspicion that the person might be at a military age. It was also possible to prove one's identity showing an employment book. Emigration procedures were also free from any additional administrative barriers. However, if a citizen was planning a permanent emigration, he could apply for so-called "emigration certificate", which resulted in a loss of the Austrian citizenship.

During the constitutional period in Austria, any attempts to legally regulate emigration issues – drafts of 1904, 1908, 1913 – proved unsuccessful. At the same time the emigration statutory law was in force and binding in Hungary[7] as well as in many other Euro-

---

[4] In the constitutional period there were three statutes that regulated this problem, and specifically those of: 5. 12. 1868 (R.G.Bl. Nr 151), of 11. 04. 1889 (R.G.Bl. Nr 41) and of 5. 07. 1912 (R.G.Bl. Nr 128).

[5] The Circular of Governor-Generalship of 25. 04. 1914 l. 9357/pr. National Archives in Cracow, collection of records C.k. Directorate of Police in Cracow (K.u.k. Polizei-Direktion in Krakau), 1852–1918 (1926), call no.: DPKr 125.

[6] R.G.Bl. Nr 116. The problems referring to passports were entirely regulated in the proclamation of 10. 05. 1867 (R.G.Bl. Nr 80).

[7] This was the Statute of 1903. For more details see: J. Puskás, *From Hungary to the United States (1880–1914)*, Budapest 1982, chapt. *The Hungarian government's emigration policy*, pp. 97ff. In its English

pean countries. The freedom to emigrate, which was guaranteed in the Act of the highest standing, namely the Constitution, was an undoubtedly modern approach. However, lack of an emigration Act had an adverse influence on the activity of government organs by creating permanent uncertainty and suspense regarding interpretation of the existing regulations. Additionally, the lack of appropriate regulations which would secure emigrants made them vulnerable to dishonest emigration agents. Partial solutions, such as the Act of 1897 mentioned below, proved unsatisfactory. Despite these facts and thanks to liberal constitutional regulations, mass earning emigration from the Polish territories under the Austrian annexation was made possible and it developed to a great extent at the turn of the 19th century.

2. The Role of Emigration Agencies in Organising Earning Emigration from Galicia

The earning emigration from Galicia in the second half of the 19th century and at the beginning of the 20th century had a form of a temporary emigration (so-called "seasonal labour"), most often to western Europe and North America, as well as permanent (settlement) emigration, especially to both Americas.[8] In both cases a great organisational role was played by emigration agencies.

Back in the 19th century it happened that emigrants leaving the country had no assistance whatsoever, either during the travel or at their destination. It regards the situation when emigrants had no guaranteed contractual work – which was the case in Europe[9] – or even any purchased boarding card (*Schiffskarte*). However, in the course of time, the emigration was more often organized with someone's intermediation. At the beginning of the "emigration rush", i.e. in the second half of the 19th century, persons well-known in their environment such as inn-keepers, merchants and even minor clerks, proved helpful for those leaving the country. It is too early to speak of the phenomenon of "organisation of emigration" since the activity of the aforementioned persons was most often exclusively limited to boarding cards trade or informal "arrangement" of employment in agricultural or industrial sectors in the West.[10] At some point, however, emigration

---

translation the Statute is published in the Internet: www.iarelative.com/hung1903/law_1903.htm The Statute was replaced by the new one in 1909. The text of the Statute accompanied by the executive act is published [in:] *Die Auswanderungsgesetzgebung. Bd. II. Die wichtigsten Europäischen Auswanderungsgesetze (mit Berücksichtigung der beiden österreichischen Entwürfe) und ihre wichtigsten Vollzugsvorschriften*, gesammelt, bezw. übersekt von F. von Srbik, Wien 1911, pp. 29ff.

[8] This problem has recently been discussed [in:] D. Praszałowicz, K.A. Makowski, A.A. Zięba, *Mechanizmy zamorskich migracji łańcuchowych w XIX wieku: Polacy, Niemcy, Żydzi, Rusini. Zarys problemu*, Kraków 2004 and [in:] A. Walaszek, *Migracje Europejczyków 1650–1914*, Kraków 2007, see also the literature listed in it.

[9] This was different in case of the United States of America. According to the emigration law that was in force in the USA the arrival of the individuals who already signed a labour contract was prohibitted. Yet it happened sometimes that in their conversation with the American officer, the emigrants, while thinking that this increases their chance to be admitted to the USA, claimed (contrary to the truth) that their employment is was already guaranteed. As a result they were often forcibly sent back to Europe.

[10] In fact already by that time there functioned larger institutions that professionally sold ship tickets. What testifies to this is a well known case referred to as the *Wadowice trial* that was held before the Circuit Court in Wadowice in November 1889. As many as 66 individuals were those who were accused in this trial.

developed to such a great extent that the institutions organising emigration were emerging spontaneously; their official task was to provide every help necessary to emigrants, including their leaving the country. These comprised emigration societies, shipping companies offices, emigration agencies, travel offices, humanitarian associations, etc. It must be pointed out though, that despite various names and legal bases of their activity, all of them were profit institutions. Even so-called humanitarian organisations made profits on emigrants. In all cases a ruthless war over intermediation in emigration broke out as it brought huge profits at that time.

The institutions that dealt with the organisation of emigration presented certain characteristics including the following:
- carrying out advertising activities, i.e. spreading among the local society information regarding advantages associated with a given company, or even conducting "emigration propaganda";
- taking care of a potential emigrant from the moment of his decision to leave the country, mainly regarding giving various instructions associated with emigration itself, legal issues, etc.;
- publishing or distributing materials such as brochures on emigration to a particular country, guide-books for emigrants, folders, price lists, timetables etc.;
- extended organisational structure including agencies, affiliates, branches, all subject to the headquarters;
- specific legal status.

Local companies with provincially-located business activity usually constituted a part of a larger whole. They could be autonomous, however, if they were directly subject to a company with a seat located outside the monarchy, e.g. in Germany.

In their business activity, the emigration organising institutions made use of their local representatives, i.e. emigration agencies. At the turn of the 19th century, both in the source literature and magazines, persons working for shipping companies and trading with boarding cards were defined as an "agent", "deputy" or "representative", and the office as an "agency", "deputation", "representation", "side office"; in the general press more abrupt definitions appeared, such as a "blood-sucker", "sponger" or "emigration hyena".[11]

Emigration agents acting at the beginning of the 20th century in Galicia could fall into the following categories:
- those acting legally (officially);
- those acting illegally (unofficially; "hole-and-corner" agents);

They were the owners and the employees of the agency engaged in the sale of the ship tickets in Oświęcim ("Jakub Klausner and Co.").

[11] The individuals engaged in this business were decidedly condemned because of the large scale of swindles commited to the prejudice of the emigrants who most frequently were the peasants. Even in the research paper they were described in this way: "the entire gang of individuals who are avaricious, without any job and of no scruples, recruited from various social strata, are busy selling the ship tickets ... In almost every small town there may be found at present some confidential individual, often occupying some lower autonomous post or that of governmental officer, wójt etc., who facilitates the making of down payments for the ship tickets needed by the emigrants", A. Benis, *Emigracya*, [in:] *IV. Zjazd Prawników i Ekonomistów Polskich. Referaty*, Kraków 1906, p. 32.

and:
- Austrian shipping companies agents (Austro-Americana line);
- foreign shipping companies agents (German, Dutch, English):
    licensed in Austria (e.g. Canadian Pacific Railway Company) or
    those without a license ("banned").

Agents made use of so-called "subagents" or "touts", whose role was limited to recruitment of potential emigrants and supplying them to the agent or a travel agency. There the emigrants were sold boarding cards. The touts were remunerated with a commission for each emigrant arriving at the agency, they did not charge the emigrants themselves, though. The touts often operated at railway stations, selecting travellers getting off trains with larger amounts of personal belongings, i.e. those who looked like those who were planning to leave the country. According to press releases, at larger stations, for example in Cracow, there were often violent incidents, including tussles between the touts of competitive emigration agencies.

In practice, there was a very small difference between the roles of an agent, subagent or a tout. Their priority was to sell as many boarding cards to the emigrants as possible. Therefore the agents often had recourse to dishonest emigration propaganda; they persuaded lower social class persons, such as poor peasants, into emigrating with the use of deceit and presentation of unreal life conditions overseas. In order to stop that disgraceful procedure and save emigrants from any abuse by emigration agents, a special Act was passed in 1897, initiated by Polish Members of the Vienna Parliament, *on criminal procedures regarding occupation with emigration issues.*[12] The Act provided for prison penalties and fines imposed on those who occupied themselves with the emigration issues without an appropriate license and for persuading into emigrating via presenting false information or "enticing into emigrating with other means". In practica, however, the norms of the Act were massively infringed while penal prosecution was scarce.

At the end of the 19th and at the beginning of the 20th centuries the whole Galicia was covered by a net of legal and hole-and-corner agents, as well as touts associated with them. Mutual relationships within these structures were truly complicated. It happened that an official agent of a licensed shipping company was at the same time a secret agent of a company without a license, or an illegal agent (i.e. a tout) worked for an official emigration organisation, etc. Agents, however, always had some sort of connection, even an indirect one, with a shipping company. Hole-and-corner agents often rendered their additional "services" such as supplying counterfeit travelling documents for recruits or helping them to cross the border.

3. The Most Important Emigration Organising Institutions Operating in Galicia

Although the activity of emigration organising institutions covered the whole of Galicia, their headquarters were situated in Cracow. The activities of various emigration agencies bore numerous similarities in their methods as well as in their internal organisation. The

---

[12] *Gesetz vom 21. Jänner 1897, womit strafrechtliche Bestimmungen in Bezug auf das Betreiben der Auswanderungsgeschafte erlassen werden* (R.G.Bl. Nr 27).

agents operating both legally and illegally applied a similar mechanism while sending emigrants overseas. They charged advance money for boarding cards and then, having received an appropriate card from the central office, they sold them to the emigrants, and collected their commission. Additionally, they provided instructions with reference to the journey, and in case of male travellers, to the required documents serving as a proof of settled military service duty. The problem of "organisation of emigration" by emigration agents was associated with both temporary and permanent emigration. In the former one, negotiating employment contracts for workers, especially in the agricultural sector, was a primary issue; in the latter – overseas transportation arrangements, especially the sale of boarding cards. The transportation included not only the journey to America itself, but also transfer to one of the European ports, often sleep-overs during the trip, accommodation at the port before the departure of a ship as well as ticket reservation for a train in America. Emigrants had to pay huge sums of money to the agents for these services.

Among an extensive number of various institutions which organised emigration, as well as emigration agencies operating in Galicia there are a few which could be listed as the most significant ones. Polish Emigration Society (Polskie Towarzystwo Emigracyjne; PTE) was established at the turn of the year 1907, it started its activity in the following year, though, having moved its seat from Lvov to Cracow. Józef Okołowicz was in charge of its works for the whole period of its existence. Polish Emigration Society was an organisation functioning according to the Act of 9th April, 1873[13] and it additionally held licenses granted to it by the authorities which allowed it to run an employment agency and a travel office. This Society was the biggest emigration institution in Galicia and it conducted intensive business activity. It had numerous affiliates across Galicia as well as abroad (in France). It published a few magazines, guide books for the emigrants, conversation manuals, as well as it supported a shelter for emigrants in Cracow. Polish Emigration Society co-operated with a number of shipping companies and travel offices, mainly with German ones. At the end of the year 1913 its activity was interrupted by the criminal proceedings instituted against the management of the Society which was suspected of commiting emigration offences.

Austro-Americana (A-A) was the most significant Austrian shipping company. The Emperor's patent of 26th November, 1852 on associations[14] as well as commercial code constituted its base of activity. In accordance with the rescript of the Ministry of Trade of 30th April, 1904, A-A was the only shipping company which had an exclusive right to set up agencies on the entire territory of the Habsburg monarchy. A-A agents were obliged to sell boarding cards only for the ships sailing out from the port in Triest and heading for America. In practice this regulation was often infringed, as the agents commonly traded in boarding cards of German, Dutch or English shipping companies. *Goldlust et Comp.* owned by Zygmunt Resch from 1911 was the general agency of Austro-Americana for the territory of Galicia and Bukowina. Its official seat was in Cracow.

Canadian Pacific Railway Company (CPRC) started its operation in 1908 in Austria, where it recruited workers for railway line construction in Canada and transported emi-

---

[13] R.G.Bl. Nr 70.
[14] R.G.Bl. Nr 253.

grants on its own ships to America.[15] CPRC operated in Austria on the basis of the ministerial license of 8th June 1908 granted in accordance with the regulation of 29th November 1865.[16] A special ministerial permission to officially operate in Galicia was granted to CPRC on 13th January, 1913. The Austrian headquarters were located in Vienna, whereas the main affiliates for the Galicia territory were opened in Cracow and Lvov. Zygmunt Gargas was in charge of the Cracow office.

Apart from the Austro-American and Canadian Pacific Railway Companies, the list of shipping companies that operated in Galicia and those that rendered their services to Polish emigrants included: Norddeutscher Lloyd, Hamburg-America (Hapag), Holland-America, Red-Star. White-Star, Cunard, Compagnie Generale Transatlantique. At the same time the foreign, and above all German, travel offices that were most active in Galicia were the following: F. Missler of Brema,[17] Karesch & Stotzky of Brema, Falck & Company of Hamburg, B. Karlsberg of Hamburg, M. Morawetz of Hamburg, M.G. Freudberg of Antverp, Vaterland of Rotterdam.

4. Conclusions

The constitutional period in Austria witnessed the guaranteed undisturbed freedom to emigrate based on the provisions of the December Constitution. At the same time, however, no legal Acts of legislative importance, which would regulate the emigration issues and functioning of emigration institutions in a comprehensive way, were binding. Temporary attempts such as the Act of 1897 proved unsatisfactory for the protection of emigrants against abuse by dishonest agents.

At the turn of the 19th century the emigrants leaving the country often relied on services of emigration institutions. Their activity left extensive material evidence. These institutions conducted advertising campaigns on a large scale, where they distributed a great variety of publishings, such as shipping companies advertisements, timetables of ships, price lists, leaflets, posters. These publishings included information, often essential to emigrants, regarding the American countries, especially referring to immigration law of the United States or South American countries.[18] During such campaigns, however, an illegal and dishonest emigration propaganda was carried out.

---

[15] On the history of Canadian Pacific Railway see: H.A. Innis, *A History of the Canadian Pacific Railway*, London–Toronto 1923; J.M. Gibbon, *The Romantic History of the Canadian Pacific Railway. The Northwest Passage of Today*, New York 1937; W.K. Lamb, *History of the Canadian Pacific Railway*, New York 1977. On the activities of Canadian Pacific in the field of emigrant transportation see: G. Musk, *Canadian Pacific. The Story of the Famous Shipping Line*, Toronto 1981. Interesting information on various aspects of the company's activities may be found in the study by D.L. Jones, *Tales of the CPR*, Calgary 2002.

[16] R.G.Bl. Nr 127.

[17] Also many Hungarian emigrants used to leave their country while using the Missler agency, see: J. Puskás, *op.cit.*, p. 102.

[18] A lot of materials published by the emigration agences could be seen at the exhibition: *Wychodźstwo z Galicji. Kraków – centrum organizacji ruchu emigracyjnego na przełomie XIX i XX wieku*, Biblioteka Jagiellońska, listopad 2003 – styczeń 2004. More details on that may be found in the exhibition catalogue (Kraków 2003). See also G.M. Kowalski, *Wydawnictwa galicyjskich instytucji organizujących wychodźstwo w zbiorach Biblioteki Jagiellońskiej*, "Biuletyn Biblioteki Jagiellońskiej" R. LVI/VII, 2006/2007, pp. 133–143.

In the course of conducted business activity, emigration agents often broke the law and resorted to so-called "emigration offence", which in most cases consisted in instigating as well as aiding and abetting on occasion of facilitating the conscripts to leave the country. That was the infringement of the provisions of the Acts regulating military service. Moreover, emigration agents massively infringed the provisions of the Act of 1897 on ban on getting involved in emigration issues without a required permit and persuading into emigration with the use of false information. The agents permanently violated licenses for the trade in boarding cards and for the running of employment agencies. They committed frauds to the detriment of emigrants and were responsible for other abuses.

Criminal court cases against the agents who were breaking the law were quite scarce in Galicia and even if the legal proceedings were conducted, the punishments were low. Due to excessive lengthiness of court proceedings, a quick and effective procedure executed by administrative organs was a commonly applied method against emigration abuse. Administrative sanctions, however, did not pose a serious threat. The most weighty criminal suits against officials of the biggest emigration institutions in Galicia began in 1913 before the National Criminal Court in Cracow. These were the cases against the management and the agents of Polish Emigration Society, Austro-Americana and Canadian Pacific Railway Company.[19] The outbreak of the war soon interrupted the proceedings. After the First World War, in the restored Republic of Poland, the proceedings were discontinued.

Constitutional Liberty in the Area of Emigration in Austria (1867–1918). The Activities of the Emigration Agencies in Galicia and Lodomeria

Summary

The law that was in force in Austria in the constitutional period guaranteed a large spectre of rights and liberties of man and citizen. Among them there was also the emigration freedom. The constitutional law of 21 Dec. 1867 *on the citizens' universal rights* provided that from the perspective of the State the emigration freedom was limited only by the duties arising from military service. Likewise, it provided that the emigration fees might be collected exclusively on the basis of the rule of reciprocity. In Galicia of the second part of the 19th century and in the early 20th century the economic emigration involving large number of individuals could be classified either as temporal (seasonal) emigration, most frequently oriented toward the West of Europe and toward North America, or as a permanent emigration, oriented particularly toward both parts of America. In both types of emigration these were the emigration agencies that played a significant role

---

¹⁹ These proceedings were discussed in the monograph by G.M. Kowalski, *Przestępstwa emigracyjne w Galicji 1897–1918... op.cit., passim.*

in organizing it. Prior to World War I the most important Galician agencies included: the Polish Emigration Society, the Austro-Americana and the Canadian Pacific Railway Company. While engaged in their business, the emigration agents constantly infringed the law by committing so called "emigration offenses". These offenses in most cases assumed the form of the instigation as well as the aiding and abetting as committed on occasion of facilitating the conscripts to leave the country. In addition, the emigration agents in massess infringed the provisions of 1897 law which prohibited dealing with the emigration matters without the required permission. The agents frequently infringed the license that was required for trading with the ship tickets. Likewise, they were responsible for swindles committed to the prejudice of the emigrants as well as for other abuses. In Galicia, the penal proceedings against the agents who broke the law were hardly ever instituted, and if ever they were the punishments imposed on the offenders were low. Due to the long-drawn-out court proceedings in case of emigration abuses, the method commonly exploited to suppress them was the prompt and effective procedure applied by the administrative organs.

Il. 1. Boarding card of the Polish Emigration Society, 1911. APKr, SKKKr 531.

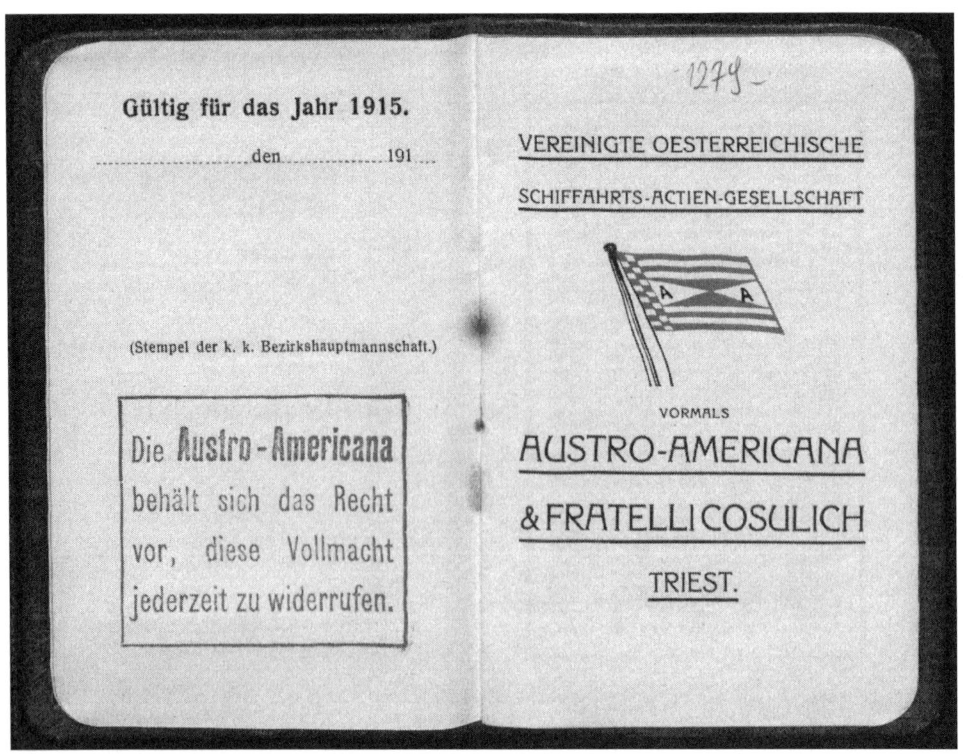

Il. 2. Identity card of an agent employed by the Austro-Americana, 1905. APKr, SKKKr 493.

AUSTRO-AMERICANA

Dampfer-Ankunft

Laut heute erhaltener Kabeldepesche ist Post- (Schnell-) Dampfer

„ *Alain* "

der am *13/2* abgegangen ist, am *27/2*

in *New York* wohbehalten

eingetroffen.

Wir bitten Sie davon die Anverwandten der gereisten Passagiere zu verständigen und zeichnen, Ihre weiteren flotten Zuweisungen erwartend,

hochachtungsvoll

General-Agentur
DER AUSTRO-AMERICANA
GOLDLUST & Co.

SKKKr 509   *673*

AUSTRO-AMERYKANA

Przybycie parowca

Wedle dzisiaj otrzymanej kablowej depeszy parowiec pocztowy

(pospieszny) ....

który odpłynął dnia .... przybył szczęśliwie dnia ....

do ....

Prosimy o zawiadomienie o tem krewnych tych pasażerów, którzy tym parowcem jechali i kreślimy się w oczekiwaniu dalszych pasażerów

z wysokiem poważaniem

AUSTRO-AMERYKANA
Jenéralna ajencya dla Galicyi i Bukowiny
GOLDLUST i Ska.

Il. 3. Austro-Americana. The information on the arrival of a steamer. APKr, SKKKr 509.

II. 4. Time-table of the Canadian Pacific Railway Company, 1913. APKr, SKKKr 536.

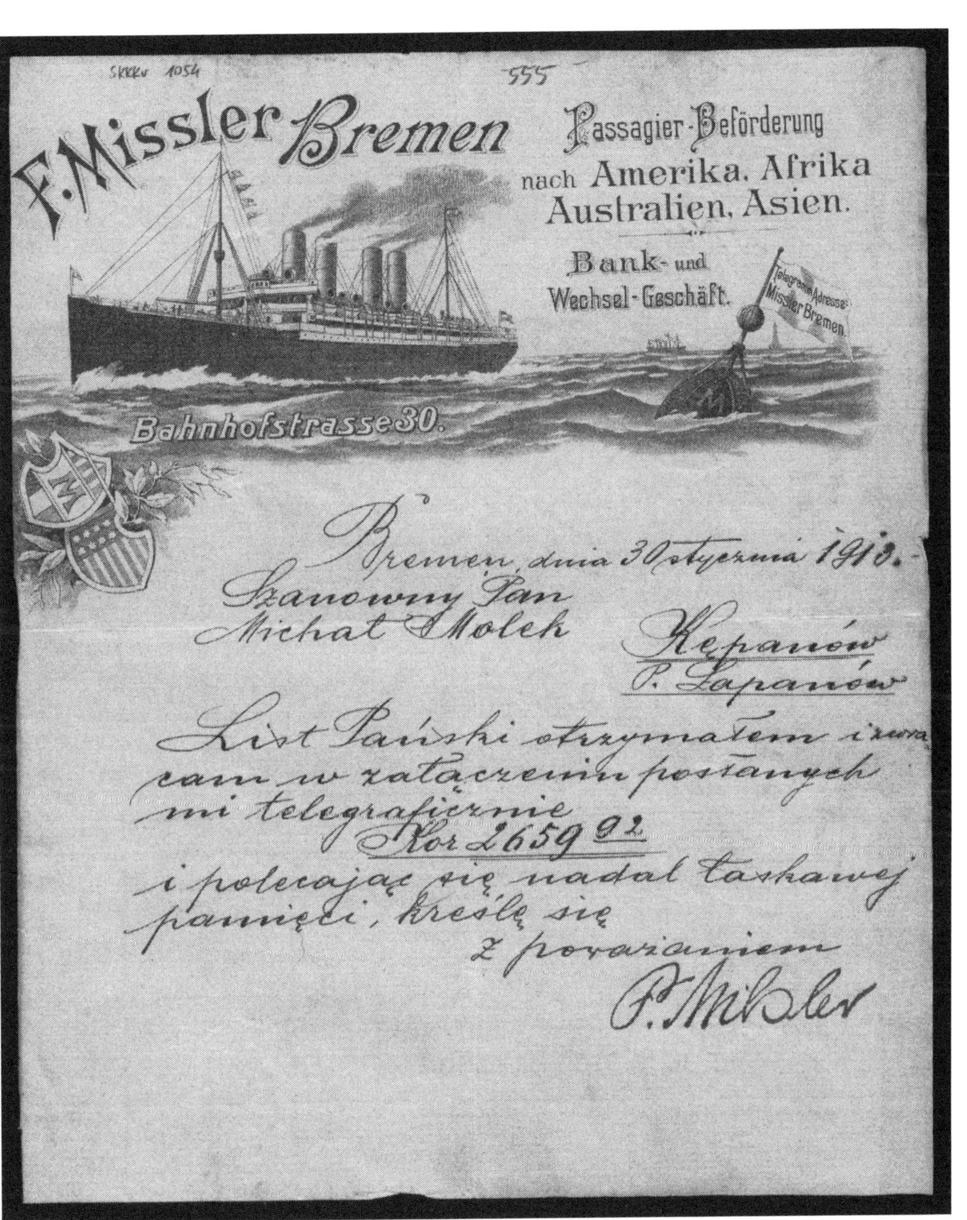

Il. 5. F. Missler's Travel Agency in Brema. Correspondence dated 1913. APKr, SKKKr 1054.

Podróżni naszą Linią do Kanady lub do New-Yorku mają następujące korzyści:

1. Nasze parowce odchodzą dwa razy na tydzień do New-Yorku i Kanady — nie ma przeto potrzeby czekać przy wodzie.

2. U nas można nabyć bilety kolejowe wprost ze Lwowa aż do wody, oraz do wszystkich miast w Ameryce i Kanadzie, tak, że nigdzie już takowych kupować nie potrzeba.

Po otrzymaniu zadatku w kwocie 20 Kor. wysyłamy szyfkartę wraz pouczeniem do podróży.

Do Ameryki północnej płaci się taksę amerykańską 20 Kor. od osoby.

Ceny są:

Hamburg—New-York (pospiesznymi parowcami)	198 172	Kor.
Hamburg—New-York (pocztowymi parowcami)	172	„
Hamburg—Argentyna	166	„
Hamburg—Filadelfia	166	„
Hamburg—Kanada	166	„

(Zmiany zastrzega się).

Il. 6. Time-table of the liners travelling between Hamburg and America. 1913, APKr, SKKKr 536.

Marian Małecki

Le roi manqué de Pologne – Stéphane II Habsburg

L'histoire de deux nations : polonaise et hongroise a connu plusieurs cas de la transition mutuelle des cours de la monarchie et des parentés entre-dynasties. Les Hongrois avaient Władysław Warneńczyk ou bien Ludwik Jagiellonczyk, les Polonais avaient Jadwiga Andegawenka et Stéphane Batory. Cet homme politique très adroit et « pas peint », comme ce souverain parlait de lui-même, pour les Polonais est un symbole du déclin « du siècle d'or » et d'une position puissante de la République de noblesse. Dans ce temps – là « beaucoup finissait »[1].

Après des siècles l'histoire a tracé un cercle. Quand la Pologne revenait sur les pages de l'histoire européenne, c'était un autre Stéphane qui devait faire revivre une ancienne puissance de la République, bien qu'il comprit des problèmes de la Pologne dans la même façon.

C'était le descendant de Marie Thérèse, Stéphane Karol Habsburg, le prince à Żywiec. Si on avait réussi de le mettre sur le trône dans les années de la Première Guerre Mondiale, il aurait été Stéphane II.

Ce héros est né en 1860 comme fils de Karol Ferdynand von Habsburg. Son oncle paternel, Albrecht Fréderic, ne laissant aucun descendant a donné ses terres au frère Karol Ferdynand. Celui – ci les a partagés entre ses fils, dont Karol Stéphane a réçu les terres à Żywiec, dans la région de Małopolska (à ce temps – là c'était la Galicié). Notre héros, dit- dessus, agrandissait et développait ces terres à tel point que vers 1918 leur surface à Żywiec s'est élévée au nombre de 53.263 hectares. Les terres agrandissaient, Karol Stéphane faisait ses activitées de philanthrope parmi les habitants du territoire de Żywiec. Il y participait à partir du moment quand la Pologne est devenue indépendante.[2]

En 1923 le prince a donné aux emigrés de la Silésie de Cieszyn qui se sont trouvés sur le territoire du pays de Tchécoslovaquie, 15 hectares de terre.

Un an après on a transmis à l'Académie de Sciences à Cracovie des terres Sporysz, Stary Żywiec, Lipowa, Jawiszowice i Brzeszcze, la partie de Dankowice (terrains voisins), Kaniów, Bestwinka, Czaniec Skidzin, Przecieszyn, Wilkowice, Grojec, Komoro-

---

[1] Comp. par exemple en langue polonais K. Olejnik, *Władysław Warneńczyk (1424–1444)*, Kraków 2007; A. Klubówna, *Królowa Jadwiga*, Warszawa 1990; sur la theme le roi Bathory K. Olejnik, *Stefan Batory (1533–1586)*, Warszawa 1988.

[2] Comp. *Księżna. Wspomnienia o polskich Habsburgach. Z Marią Krystyną Habsburg rozmawiali: Adam Tracz, Krzysztof Błecha*, Żywiec 2009, p. 8.

wice, Bark, la partie de Bestwina, Cięcina, Lipnik et Bulowice (près de Wadowice). Une vraie aubaine pour l'Académie c'eétait le don des forêts aux environs de la montagne Babia Góra, de la surface de 6.795 hectares. Le pays polonais a réçu le palais à Rajcza pour y créer le sanatorium. Ces donnations sont importantes mais ce ne sont pas les seules offres faites par cet homme extraordinaire. Après sa mort en 1933, ces biens (terres) étaient partagés entre les enfants du prince.

Karol Stéphane s'est fait connaitre comme navigateur, passionné pour ce sport, naviguant à CK dans la Marine de Guerre, à l'âge de 35 ans et il a décidé de s'installer pour toujours sur le territoire de Żywiec. Nous ne connaissons pas la vraie cause de cette décision. Peut-être c'est le paysage pittoresque de ce lieu (forêts, montagnes, paysage ressemblant un peu aux terrains dans les Alpes, en Autriche) qui l'a poussé au choix de Żywiec.

Pendant son séjour dans cette ville, l'archiduc a fait agrandir, surtout le château à Żywiec, en lui donnant une fonction représentative. Alors en 1898 il a bâti une annexe, du côté du sud du château, en 1908–1909 il a bâti une chapelle et un bâtiment octogone lié avec un volume(bloc) du palais, cela veut dire, un bandeau. Le château, on dit la perle de l'histoire, est conservé jusqu'aux nos temps. La partie de l'est du château a été transformée en 1911 et sur ryzalit (façade un peu avancée du château) on a placé le signe d'origine de la dynastie de Habsburg.

La journée quotidienne de la famille d'archiduc se passait d'après une étiquette du cour de la dynastie de Habsburg. Le rythme de la journée était aussi indiqué par l'éducation des enfants : l'apprentissage de cinq langues (polonais, allemand, italien, français, anglais), matières exactes, histoire d'art.[3]

La journée commencait par la messe dans la chapelle (7.00 du matin en été et 7.30 en hiver) et le petit déjeuner léger avec du café et « sztrudel » autrichien (une charlotte). Ensuite les cours des enfants, les affaires liées avec la gestion du patrimoine, la réception des invités. Vers du 10 heures du matin, on disait, le deuxième petit déjeuner, on se servait des tartines et un verre de vin.[4]

Vers du midi les membres de la famille dirigeaient leurs pas vers leurs chambres pour changer et puis venir au déjeuner, que l'on prenait avec une certaine cérémonie.

Après le déjeuner l'archiduc et son épouse avaient le temps libre pendant lequel on jouait au tennis, on faisait des randonnées dans le parc, on pêchait, on faisait du patin à roulettes.

Après 16 heures on servait le goûter, le plus souvent on le servait sur l'une des terrasse, c'étaient du thé, des biscuits ou bien des fruits.

Après le lunch, les enfants participaient aux cours pour qu'ils puissent manger, on disait le deuxie ème déjeuner ou plutôt le dîner. Après le repas, les membres de la famille allaient se reposer.

Aux mois d'hiver la dynastie de Habsburg venant de Żywiec, partait souvent pour la Croatie, sur l'île Losinj, où leur possession se trouvait.

Les Habsburgs, depuis du début essayaient de créer de bonnes relations avec une aristocratie polonaise, dont l'exemple le plus significatif est le mariage de leur fille

---

³ *Ibidem*, pp. 24–25.

⁴ *Ibidem*.

Maria Renata[5] qui a épousé Hieronim Radziwiłł.[6] En 1909 le mariage était réussi et c'était le mariage d'amour, le choix du coeur de la part de Marie Renata, ce qui était rare dans la famille de Habsburg.[7] L'autre fille, Mathilde[8] en 1913 épouse le duc Olgierd Czartoryski.[9]

Karol Stéphane reconnaissait bien les Polonais (il ne les nommait pas les Galiciens, comme essayait de le faire son ancêtre Joseph II), c'est grâce à la participation au parlement et au gouvernement autrichien.

Presque pendant une décade le professeur de l'Université Jagiellone, Julien Dunajewski a exercé la fonction du ministre du trésor, c'est Leon Biliński qui l' a aussi été, mais le compte Kazimierz Badeni était à la tête du gouvernement. L'autre aristocrate Agenor due Gołuchowski jusqu'à 1906 a exercé la fonction du ministre des affaires étrangères.[10] On peut supposer que la Pologne fascinait Karol Stéphane jusqu'à tel point qu'il acceptait la polonisation du choix, en pleine conscience et d'une façon charmante.

En s'intéressant à l'histoire du territoire de Żywiec il a découvert le fait de la présence du roi de Pologne Jean II Kazimierz Waza au château de Żywiec, ce qui a été commémoré par la fondation du tableau dans le château.[11]

Ensuite il aidait la Société Gimnastique « Sokół » à Żywiec en devenant l'un de ses fondateurs. En 1914 il a réçu un appel au service militaire (depuis 1912 il exercait la fonction d'admiral de la flotte adriatique).[12]

Pour ceux qui ne connaissent pas le réel du territoire de Żywiec, le fait que les soldats da la companie de Żywiec partaient au front de combat en prononcant les mots : « vive Stéphane II, futur roi de Pologne » pourrait être choquant. Peu de temps après il a organisé le deuxième détachement de la companie de Żywiec « Sokołów ». Quand le 25 aout 1914 ils partaient vers leur destin, l'archiduc leur a adresse les paroles en polonais, en les appelant « ... a la gloire et le retour heureux, que Dieu vous garde ».

La petite-fille Maryna Radziwiłłówna faisait ses adieux aux legionnaires partant en leur donnant des oeillets rouges et blancs. Quand ils descendaient du train, au-dessus de la gare on voyait un grand portrait du roi de Pologne Stéphane Batory qui luttait contre Iwan Groźny et les Russes. L'association d'idées était claire.

La question de la Pologne aurait dû apparaitre dans les considérations des hommes poltiques. L'une des premières personnes qui ont commencé à la toucher était Julien Andrassy, Hongrois. Il parlait directement de la création du Royaume Polonais.[13]

---

[5] Maria Renata von Habsburg (1888–1935).

[6] Hieronim Radziwiłł (1885–1945), fils de Dominique Radziwiłł i Dolores d'Agramonte, une beauté espagnolle.

[7] On a permis à la fille Eléonora (1886–1974) de faire une mésalliance avec Alfon von Kloss, noble silésien qui a repondu à l'amour de sa future mais elle a été dépouillée de son héritage après Habsburgs, selon le commendement de François Joseph I.

[8] Machtylda von Habsburg (1891–1966).

[9] Olgierd Czartoryski (1888–1977), le destin l'a ammené à Rio de Janerio, où il est mort. Il est né à Sielec, dans le sud de Wielkoplska. Comp. St. Jędraś, *Miasto i gmina Jutrosin*, Leszno 1999, pp. 335–341.

[10] M. Małecki, *Diète Nationale de Galicie*, Lisboa 2010, en presse.

[11] M. Małecki, *Euroregion „Beskidy". Historia i współczesność*, Bielsko-Biała 2006, p. 187.

[12] En réalité il commendait la flotte d'admiral Anton Haus.

[13] Compar. *Grande geurre 1914–1918* sous la red. de Jan Dąbrowski, Varsovie–Cracovie 1937, p. 527.

La conception de la restitution du Royaume Polonais a eu son début sur l'arène internationale un peu plus tard, en 1916.

L'archiduc a deplacé à Pszczyna, ville éloignée à 40 kilomètres au Nord-Ouest. Ici, il y avait le siège de l'état- major de l'est de l'armée allemande, ici a séjourné l'empereur allemand Guillaume II, enfin, ici est venu l'empereur François Joseph I. Pendant les discussions assez violentes on refléchissait comment gagner une nouvelle recrue, surtout venant du territoire de la Pologne et c'était la raison pour laquelle on essayait de créer le Royaume Polonais.[14]

On ne définissait pas de frontières, même de système, sauf la constatation que cela sera une monarchie constitutionelle. Pourtant on déterminait la tendance (sens) on disait : du problème polonais. On proposait aussi des candidatures des souverains de la nouvelle monarchie.

A vrai dire on a traité sérieusement les deux : le duc de Pszczyna Jean XV von Hochberg, dont la candidature a été proposée par l'empereur Guillaume et Karol Stéphane Habsburg, dont la candidature était favorisée par les hommes politiques à Vienne.

S'il s'agît du premier, il a obtenu l'approbation, grâce a ses racines de Piaści : on dit qu'on avait du s'apparenter l'un de ses ancêtres avec l'une des princesses silésiennes de la famille de Piastowicze. En ce qui concerne le deuxième, un argument pour, c'était la polonisation, à laquelle il s'est soumis et le fait qu'il se sentait Polonais.

Nous ne connaissons pas les causes pour lesquelles l'empereur François Joseph I a résigné cette idée. Peut-être pour les raisons ambitionnelles. Le fait est que Stéphane a bien réagi contre cette candidature au contraire de son adversaire allemand.

« L'acte du 5 novembre 1916 » était très important pour la Pologne parce qu'il a internationnalisé la question de sa formation.

Il a été mis par écrit selon de différentes relations à la curé de Pszczyna et d'autres qui venaient du château de Pszczyna. Enfin il a été annoncé à tout le monde à Varsovie.

Encore une fois, pendant la conférence à Spa en 1918 on a proposé la candidature de Karol Stéphane- sans résultat. La Pologne s'est renée en ne comptant pas sur les pays centraux, vaincus et a décidé elle – même de son système.

Karol Stéphane est resté soi-même sans conviction d'être Polonais. Il n'est pas parti, au contraire, il a crée sa résidence principale à Żywiec.

Ses fils se considéraient comme Polonais : Karol Olbracht était en grade du colonel au 16 régiment d'artillerie, Léon, capitaine de cavalerie au 17 régiment d'uhlans. Seulement Guillaume luttait en Ukraine contre les Polonais, en coséquence son père lui a renoncé dans la presse.

Ses petits – enfants naissaient ; le duc vieillssait. Il est mort le 7 avril 1933 à cause de la crise du coeur, son épouse est morte le 9 mai 1933 à cause da l'arythmie du coeur.

Aujourd'hui, dans le château de Żywiec la monarchie des Habsburgs commence à revivre. C'est la petite fille du roi manqué de Pologne – Maria Cristina Habsburg qui voulait accentuer son origine polonaise comme son grand-père lui disait et elle a renoncé à « von » devant son nom.

---

[14] M. Małecki, *Les Habsourg ou les Hochberg sur le trôné polonais? La conception de former l'Etat polonais selon l'acte du 5 novembre 1916*, en *Počcta Stanislavu Baliku k 80. narozeninam*, ed. Vilem Knoll, Plzen 2008, pp. 229–235.

Karol Stefan II Habsburg, the Would-be King of Poland

Summary

In the present paper Karol Stefan von Habsburg was presented as the candidate to the throne of Poland. He was promoted to that position at the end of World War I. He was the individual who was particularly significant for the region of Żywiec. Likewise, he was the man of merit from the perspective of Polish culture to which he rendered remarkable services. The present article is a short biographical sketch of this extraordinary individual.

ZSUZSANNA PERES

The Cultural Heritage of the Hungarian Fideicommissa

Wherever we hear the word "fideicommissum" there usually appears in our mind the vision of a huge real property – as the famous Hungarian authors of the 19th century emphasized it – with a big country house, where the owner was usually resting on the porch smoking his pipe, with his dog nearby his legs, and the creaking of the well sweep was the only noise that could be heard near and far in the immense sweltering heat. This is the vision of a presently bygone world, in which the fideicommissum represented the controversial institution with its inalienable nature.

The legal authors of the 19th century seem to adopt a view that this legal institution should be erased from the legal system for the benefit of the enlightened political and legal changes. They believed that the foundation of a fideicommissum reduced the possibility of acquiring credits and prevented the making of investments in the fideicommissum property since the possessor of the fideicommissum could not be sure that by his death his family could get at least the amount of the investment back.[1] But it is also true that without this legal institution most of our present museums would be poorer. These collections and treasures that now form part of the permanent collection of the Hungarian Museum of Fine Arts, or the National Gallery in Budapest were preserved due to the fideicommissa created by Hungarian nobles living in the 17th through 18th centuries.

The cultural heritage of the Hungarian fideicommissa consists mostly of paintings, drawings or jewels that belonged to famous Hungarian noble families whose members rose from anonymity during the second half of the 17th century and grounded the economic basis of their clans. These treasures inherited by the heirs of the specific family and protected always from alienation or purchase nowadays are part of the Hungarian artistic collections because they were given as gifts or sold to these Museums by the members of the family in the 19th through 20th centuries.

A collection of paintings was sold in the second half of the 19th century when the Esterházy family suffered economic decline. To solve the problem Prince Nicholaus

---

[1] Fleischhacker János, *Institutiones Juris Hungarici, praemissis Ejusdem Historia, ac Prolegomenis Tres in Libros divisae*, Posonii 1795; Szlemenics Pál, *Elementa Juris Hungarici Civilis Privati*, Posonii 1819; Kelemen Emericus, *Institutiones Juris Hungarici Privati*, Buda 1818; Alsóviszti Fogarasi János, *Magyarhoni magános törvéntudomán elemei Kövy Sándor után újabb törvéncikkelek 's felső itéletekkel és más bővítésekkel*, Pest 1839; Kövy Alex, *Elementa Jurisprudentiae Hungaricae S. Patakini, Impressa per Andreanum Nádaskay*, 1823; Frank Ignácz, *Principia Juris Civilis Hungarici*, vol. I–II, Pestini 1829.

Esterházy III in his Letter of 15th June 1867 offered the Head of the Hungarian Academy of Science, Baron Joseph Eötvös the sale of the collection to the Hungarian state. In 1870 the contract was signed and more than 50% of the Esterházy picture-gallery was purchased by the Hungarian State for the price of 1.3 million Hungarian florins. From 1906 on, this collection forms now part of the permanent collection of the Hungarian Museum of Fine Arts.[2]

Other movables of the Esterházy fideicommissum had been transferred from Forchtenstein (nowadays Güns in Austria) to Budapest in 1919. In 1920 the contemporary fideicommissum heir, Prince Nicholaus Esterházy and Gyula Végh, the director of the Museum of Applied Arts, signed a deposit-contract that was renewed in 1923 by Prince Paul Esterházy. For the first time the Museum of Applied Arts opened the exposition of these treasures in 1924. When the Soviet troops were approaching Budapest in 1944, Prince Paul Esterházy, while trying to protect the treasury, decided to transfer the whole collection from the Museum to the Keller of his Princely Palace that was located in the Tárnok Street Nr. 7–13 in Budapest. Unfortunately this building was struck by a bomb and buried under its ruins the greatest treasure collection of modern Hungary of that time. From the 1950's the Museum started the renovation of the preserved pieces that survived the destroying of the palace.

Apart from the Esterházy collection there were also precious movables of other Hungarian noble families that arrived at the collections of the above mentioned Museums. Thus the treasures of the Thurzó, Erdődy, Zichy and Pálffy families can be seen nowadays in the museums since some of them were donated by the members of these families to the Museum in the first half of the 20th century or sold by way of auction.[3]

1. The Legislation of the Fideicommissum in the Hungarian Kingdom

The institution of fideicommissum appeared in the Hungarian legal system quite late, after the Turks had been expelled from Buda in 1686.[4] For a long time it was believed that this institution was a reward that the Hungarian aristocrats received from the Hungarian King for resigning from their right of resistance granted to them by Andrew II in the

---

[2] For more details see *Esterházy – kincsek. Öt évszázad műalkotásai a hercegi gyűjteményekből*, ed. Szilágyi András, Budapest 2006–2007 (The catalogue of the Museum of Applied Arts Budapest) p. 6 and 48; Imre Katona, *A fraknói kincstár 1725-ös leltára*, [in:] *Művészettörténeti Értesítő (1980) 2*, pp. 131–147, in this case pp. 115–133; Barkóczi István, *Az Esterházy képtár*, [in:] *Arisztokrácia, Művészetek, Mecenatúra – Kastélykonferenciák 3. Az Esterházy – család*. The presentations of the conference held on 22–23 April 2004. Keszthely 2005, ed. László Czoma, pp. 171–186, in this case pp. 183–184.

[3] In 1929 Count László Pálffy donated a precious cup belonging to the family and dating back to the end of the 16th century to the Historical Museum of Hungary. It can now be seen in the National Museum of Hungary. More details may be found in Bárányné Oberschall Magda, *Pálffy Miklós aranyserlege a Magyar Történeti Múzeumban*, [in:] *Magyar Művészet XIV.*, 1938, pp. 282–285.

[4] This fact does not mean that this institution did not have its customary legal antecedents in the Hungarian legal practice. The Hungarian nobles knew this legal institution well and they also lived with the possibility of creating "majorats" but without any legal binding force. In view of the absence of the legislative enactment the fulfilment of the testator's last will of creating "majorats" was entrusted to the discretion of the heirs. See more details in Peres Zsuzsanna, *A magyar "hitbizományi" jog kezdetei*, PhD thesis, 2009, pp. 36–94.

Golden Bull of 1222 and for electing and crowning around 10 year-old Joseph I as King of the Hungarian Kingdom in 1687.[5] But the study of the documents of the General Assembly of 1687–1688 and the family documents of the Esterházy family – whose most famous member, Paul Esterházy[6] was the Palatine of the Hungarian Kingdom at that time – allows to arrive at another conclusion. This institution was introduced because one man, a politically really influent one, the Palatine of the Hungarian Kingdom, wanted to preserve both his immovable and movable property from the negligence by his heirs.[7]

At the time when he was elected Palatine by the Diet of 1681 which was convoked in Sopron he didn't feel himself politically strong enough to accomplish his purpose. But when Leopold I convoked the Diet in 1687 to Pozsony (today Bratislava, Slovak Republic), from which he hoped to obtain the allowance for the coronation of his son Joseph and the acceptance for the transformation of the Hungarian Kingdom into a hereditary monarchy according the rules of the primogeniture Paul Esterházy also felt sufficiently strong to materialize his plans referring to the future of his family fortune.[8] The Palatine

---

[5] Králik Lajos, *Hitbizományi jogunkról – Pálffy János gróf végrendelete*, Bp. 1909, p. 8.

[6] The very interesting personality and life of the Palatine proves that, too. He was the member of the most famous noble family of the 17th to 18th centuries in Hungary. The family owned almost the whole western (so-called Trans-Danubian) parts of Hungary. Being educated in the enlightened noble court of Palatine Nicholaus Esterházy, as his third-born son, as his future heir, he was educated together with his brothers in the famous Jesuit's College of Nagyszombat (today Trnava, Slovak Republic). Because of the early death of his older brothers' (Stephan and Leslie Esterházy) he inherited one of the biggest fortune of that time at the age of 12 after he was declared major by King Ferdinand III on the 21st of October 1652. In order to protect the family fortune he, after obtaining the papal dispensation from the second-grade collateral consanguinity, married his step-brother's daughter, the eleven-year-old Ursula Esterházy. This fact had to be kept secret until the girl reached the age of 14 and came of age. Thanks to his talent and the family's good fame Paul Esterházy made speedy career in serving the King. At the climex of his political career he was elected Palatine of the Hungarian Kingdom in 1681 and obtained the title of Prince in 1687. He spent most of his life fighting against the Turks on the side of the King. In return for this he got donations from the King thereby increasing the political influence and economic basis of the family. He had an enviable personal career by being a well-educated and rich aristocrat, who knew no obstacles that could prevent him from preserving the name and fame of his noble family. Besides, he was that person who was susceptible to arts. He was a talented composer and a devoted fighter against the Protestantism. Iványi Emma, *Esterházy Pál Mars Hungaricus*, ed. Hausner Gábor, Budapest, Zrínyi Kiadó, 1989, pp. 431–438, 450; Iványi Emma, *Esterházy Pál nádor közigazgatási tevékenysége (1681–1713)*, Budapest 1991, pp. 28–30; Erdélyi Aladár, *Régi magyar családi hitbizományok története és joga (1542–1852)*, Budapest 1912, pp. 203–204; Tobler Felix, *Az Esterházy–család birodalmi hercegi méltósága*, [in:] *Arisztokrácia, Művészetek, Mecenatúra...*, pp. 38–53, in this case pp. 39–39, 44.

[7] Palatine Paul Esterházy wrote several last wills and testaments and in those that were prepared before the Act 9 of 1687 entered into force he always mentioned that the indivisibility of the family fortune is the only way of preserving the family's name and fame, and this aim can be reached only by the fideicommissum which is practiced in almost all countries of Europe. For this reason he created fideicommissum on all his property, both immovable and movable, which as he says: "seems to contradict the Hungarian laws and if his heirs do not want to fulfil his will in this subject no one can force them to do so". But he hoped that his heirs would not be persuaded by the arguments of the family's enemies and thus deterred from the fulfilment of the fideicommissum. The Palatine's testaments were published by Merényi Lajos, *Gróf Esterházy Pál 1664. évi végrendelete*, [in:] *Történelmi Tár (1911)*, Budapest, pp. 151–157; idem, *Gróf Esterházy Pál 1678. évi végrendelete*, [in:] *ibidem*, pp. 599–619; in this case p. 156 and p. 616.

[8] Bérenger Jean, Kecskeméti Károly, *Országgyűlés és parlamenti élet Magyarországon 1608–1918*, Budapest 2008, pp. 102–104; Turba Gustav, *Geschichte des Thronfolgerechtes in allen Habsburgischen Ländern bis zur Pragmatischen Sanktion Kaiser Karls VI. 1156 bis 1732*, Wien und Leipzig, 1903, pp. 355–356; idem, *Die Grundlagen der Pragmatischen Sanktion. I. Ungarn*, Leipzig–Wien, 1911, pp. 9–19.

contributed to the success of the King's court. He did it by serving as mediator between the estates of the realm and the monarch. The time-consuming debates ended in the acceptance of the hereditary rights of the Habsburgs to the throne of Hungary (in case the Austrian male line died out the Spanish line would get the Crown).[9]

Boldizsár Patachich, a deputy of the Diet, mentions in his Diary:

> it was ordered and submitted as a bill by the present Palatine among the grievances of the Estates ... that the acquisitors' of properties be allowed to create fideicommissum and majority life-interest for their children, for the preservation of their families, which prerogative became possible for the inhabitants of the country according to the rules of free disposal.[10]

This bill of the Palatine can also be found among the documents of the 1687/88 Diet.[11] Only a short response came to this bill from the King's court in the endorsement of the 13th of January 1688 in which the monarch was of opinion that the creation of fideicommissa did not contradict the King's will. In addition it was 13 years earlier that he granted this prerogative to the nobles of the Austrian Hereditary Provinces' in his letter patent of 2nd November 1674.[12] The foundation of fideicommissa did not harm the purposes of the King because their entering into effect always depended on the prerogative of the King who had to give his royal assent to their creation. The monarch hoped to pull the aristocrats to his side by donating them the reconquered territories of the country.[13]

---

[9] The parliamentary sessions lasted for five months for this reason. Máriássy Béla, *A magyar törvényhozás és Magyarország történelme, 3. kötet I. Miksától – III*, Károlyig, Győr 1887, p. 178; Goldschmiedt Kálmán, *A trónörökösödés kérdése az 1687–88.-i országgyűlésen*, Budapest 1914; Csekey István, *A magyar trónöröklési jog. Jogtörténelmi és közjogi tanulmány oklevélmellékletekkel*, Budapest 1917, pp. 107–162.

[10] "Leguntur tum residua et per Dominum Palatinum praesentim per modum projecti porrecta gravamina inter quo id etiam ut liceat aequisitoribus bonorum inter filios fideicommissum seu majorescum usu fructuarium nempe solum modo bonorum instituere pro conservatione familiae quod Regnicolis superfluum visum (est), cum sufficientes Leges liberum dispositionem admitterent." Balthasar Patachich, *Diarium et Acta Comitiorum S. Regni Hungaria*, Anno 1687 Posonii celebratorum 1687, p. 27.

[11] "Non exiguam Magnatum seu Procerum Regni familiarum experiri per Status et Ordines in eo ruinam, quod non pauci e numero earundem haeredes ac successores paterna et materna, ac paterno ex materno avitica bona absque ulla extrema necessitatis exigentia distraherent, quorum ad refraenandum prodigalitatem justo decerni, quodsi quispiam Magnatum seu Procerum de bonis sui a modo imposterum sive per servitia emeriti aut proprio marte sive ex fructibus aviticorum bonorum acquisitis per dispositionem testamentariam praevie in Comitatibus publicandam fideicommissum et majoratum fecerit, constitueritque haeredes et successores ejusdem de hujusmodi bonis nullam habeant quoad Capitale contra vim et tenorem praedeclaratae dispositionis acquisitorum praefatorum impignorandi et alienandi facultatem verum sint solummodo usufructuarii: Quod si vero quispiam mentionatorum Magnatum supra talia bona fidei utpote commissa summam aliquam pecunialem concesserit, illam (via juris in Comitatibus eorundem Judicibus per alterum fratrem in hujusmodi majoratu immediatum successorem hoc modo prosequenda) in perpetuum eo facto amittat. Praesenti nihilominus gravamine ad mentionatas duntaxat Magnates seu Proceres (quibus nimirum eatenus sic disponendi integrum fore videbitur) extendent haeredes ac successores non vero nobiles vel eorundem haeredes extenso existente." HHStA Wien Ungarn 402 Comitialia Fasc. 402. Konv. C. 1687/88.

[12] "Fideicommissa in linea descendenti constituta et a Sacrae Caesareae Majestate confirmata a successoribus sine cognitione causa in jure fundata non graventur." HHStA Wien Ungarn 402 Comitialia Fasc. 402. Konv. C. 1687/88; HHStA Wien, Staatskanzlei, Patente Kt.nr. 14 (Alt 11).

[13] The Palatine proposed the King to donate the reconquered territories to those noble families to whom they belonged before the invasion of the Turks. Kállay István, *A tulajdonviszonyok ciklikus újrarendezése Magyarországon 1686–1945*, [in:] Jogtudományi Közlöny (1993) XLVIII. évf. 4. szám. pp. 159–162, in this case

The maneuvers made by the Palatine are also supported by the comparison of the text of his several testaments with the text of the Act 9 of 1687 about the prerogative of creating fideicommissum for the aristocrats, the wording of these documents is very similar. It is also symptomatic that no large wave of fideicomissa followed. Only six families resorted to the possibility of creating them before 1723.

2. *The Creation of Aristocratic Treasure Collections*

The legislation on fideicommissa coincided with the progress of the counter-reformation that brought the art of the Baroque to the Hungarian Kingdom. The aristocrats grouped around the King felt themselves obliged to be highly devoted to the Roman Catholic religion and they manifested their devotion by making *pia causa* foundations for religious and charitable purposes. Notwithstanding this, the Baroque style of living drew the attention of the aristocrats to the artistic patronage and the genealogical family tree research. The aristocrats built huge palaces, exponential of the fortune. They collected treasures and precious movables as well as rare books. They housed them in their palaces in which they organized family libraries. For preventing the alienation of these goods they ordered them to form part of the family fideicommissa and thus become inalienable and beyond the possibility of being purchased.

The Esterházy Treasures

Palatine Nicholaus Esterházy, father of the later Palatine Paul Esterházy, was the person who started the hoarding of treasures although he became more famous by his devotion to architecture. It is his son who is considered to be the real treasure-collector. Paul Esterházy was particularly concerned with the investigation of the family genealogy. While Nicolaus depicted his family-tree down to the 12th century, his son started depicting it from Charles the Great. Later he tried to penetrate the roots of the family down to the era of Adam and Eve.[14]

Nicholaus Esterházy obtained the possession of the precious pieces thanks to his fruitful marriages. In 1611 he contracted marriage with Ursula Dersffy, the rich widow who came from Northern – Hungary and who was previously married to Captain Franciscus Mágochy. Ursula Dersffy was the heir of the famous bishop Nicholaus Oláh from whom she inherited not only his palace of Lakompach but also his huge library full of such rarities as first prints of the books by Martin Luther, Melanchton and Erasmus of Rotterdam. The oldest book of the *Bibliotheca Esterházyana* was published in 1482 in

---

p. 160; The King treated the Hungarian Kingdom as a territory conquered by his armed forces where he could rule without observing the traditional Hungarian constitution. Bartoniek Emma, *A magyar királykoronázások története; A magyar Történelmi Társulat könyvei IV.*, Budapest 1939, p. 96, Iványi (quot. 6), p. 446; Szita János, *Magyarország és a Habsburg – tartományok kapcsolata 1526 és 1847 között*, [in:] *Degré Alajos emlékkönyv*, ed. Máthé Gábor, Zlinszky János, Budapest 1995, pp. 313–333, in this case p. 315.

[14] Paul Esterházy had the "Trophaeum nobilissimae familiae Esterhazyanae" printed in 1700 in which he collected all the real and legendary ancestors of his family. Buzási Enikő, *Képmás és mintakép. Az Esterházy–ősgaléria képi forrásai*, [in:] *Arisztokrácia, Művészetek, Mecenatúra…*, pp. 159–171, in this case p. 161.

Venice.[15] Apart from the library also other precious movables such as carpets and jewels came to the Esterházy family with this marriage. After his wife's death and five years of widowhood Nicholaus Esterházy decided to marry again. This time he selected as his wife Christine Nyáry, the widow of the very rich Emericus Thurzó. Upon this marriage he was granted the tutorship of the Thurzó female orphan whom he soon married with his firstborn son Stephan Esterházy. Their child, Ursula Esterházy, inherited the whole Thurzó fortune that became part of the Esterházy fortune from then on. Together with the new wife some unique golden cups and other pieces of artworks became incorporated to the treasury. Among them there were inter alia a golden cup worth of 450 gulden made by Hans Petzolt for Mathias II who gave it as a present to Emericus Thurzó on occasion of one of his visits, and some precious gold pendants and the so called "poison ring" of Stanislaus Thurzó, the bishop of Olomutz, the ring dating back to the 16th century.[16]

The treasury accumulated by Nicholaus Esterházy contained also some Turkish pieces, among them a worthy golden silver flag-point as the most precious loot of that time seized from Pasha Ibrahim Sokolovith in 1623 by Nicholaus Esterházy when he was Captain of fortress Érsekújvár.[17] While enlarging his collection of works of art, Nicholaus Esterházy decided to rebuild two rooms of his Castle of Forchtenstein for purposes of keeping the treasury there.[18]

Also the first pieces of the Esterházy picture – gallery came from that time. This was the time when the first noble portraits started to be painted. The phenomenon of painting portraits appeared first in the 1570s. It became popular mostly among the secular and clerical high-officials of the King's court. At the beginning of the 17th century this tendency reached the mannieristic court of Prague. The first oil-painting portraits of Hungarian noble family members appeared in the 1610s. The sons of Nicholaus Esterházy were brought up in such a millieu that was susceptible to arts. They cherished the fashion that mirrored the aristocratic courtly culture.[19]

In his testament, Palatine Nicholaus Esterházy ordered his movables to follow the legal status of these castles and palaces where they were kept and to be divided among his three sons and two daughters. Even if he said in his testament that he was not in possession of a big movable fortune, from the inventory made at his death in 1645 we can find that his treasury was by no means as poor as the modest Palatine said.[20]

After Nicholaus Esterházy's death a lot of inventories were prepared, particularly during the life of Palatine Paul Esterházy. These inventories testify to the efforts made for

---

[15] Gabriel Theresia, *Egy mozgalmas múlt tanúja – a herceg Esterházy – könyvtár*, [in:] *Arisztokrácia, Művészetek, Mecenatúra...*, pp. 76–91, in this case p. 77.

[16] Szilágyi (quot. nr. 2), pp. 18–22.

[17] Pásztor Emese, *Die osmanisch – türkischen Objekte in der Esterházy – Schatzkammer*, [in:] *Von Bildern und anderen Schätzen. Die Sammlungen der Fürsten Esterházy*, ed. Galavics Géza, Mraz Gerda, Wien 1990, pp. 83–99, in this case p. 83.

[18] Szilágyi (quot. nr. 2), pp. 24–25.

[19] Galavics Géza, *Die Frühen Porträts der Familie Esterházy. Typen, Funktion, Bedeutung – eine Auswahl (Ein Forschungsbericht)*, [in:] *Adelige Hofhaltung im österreichisch – ungarischen Grenzraum. Vom Ende des 16. bis zum Anfang des 19. Jahrhunderts*, ed. Kropf Rudolf, Schlag Gerald, Eisenstadt 1998, pp. 105–125, in this case p. 107, 110.

[20] The inventory of 1645 was published by Kálmán Thaly. Thaly Kálmán, *Gr. Eszterházy Miklós nádor kincstára (1645)*, [in:] *Történelmi Tár*, 1883, pp. 755–767.

the enrichment of the family-treasury. These inventories sometimes were written by the Palatine himself who with great accuracy described each piece of art. These inventories are of great value for the present day art historians.[21]

The treasures dating back to the time of Paul Esterházy can be divided into different groups. The first treasury to be mentioned is the one that contained jewels, guns, goldsmith's and silversmith's works, wall carpets and such rarities as a golden-silvered griffin's claws or the prepared crocodile that is hanging until now at the portico of the Castle of Forchtenstein.[22] A part of these movables can also be nowadays found in the Esterházy ancient place, where Nicholaus Esterházy ordered them to be kept. Nowadays they are sometimes transferred to different Museums for exhibitions. The second group contained the collection of paintings and drawings that were mainly accumulated by Nicholaus Esterházy II at the end of the 18th century. From 1794 until 1833 he collected 1156 paintings, 3500 drawings and 50.000 engravings.[23] The third group consists of the books of the Bibliotheca Esterházyana. The details about the content of the library can be found in the catalogue dated 1725: *Catalogus Librorum in Arce et Bibliotheca Frakno repositorum.*[24] The 27 pages of the catalogue in form of the 595 books that make up the library. Most of the books were written in Latin but there were some German, Greek, Italian and French books, too. According to this catalogue there were: 63 ecclesiastical and historical books; 348 of them were purely ecclesiastical, 334 *haeretici*, 160 scholastic, 49 juridical, 100 medical, 220 political and historical, 17 books were about the military and the geometry, 2 about the history of animals, 3 were botanical, 70 of ancient prays, 16 of astrology, mathematics and chemistry, 50 of geography, 47 about topography and 17 about hydrographs.[25]

Paul Esterházy ordered his library to be given to the Franciscans where the educated scholars of that time could enjoy reading them. He restrained the alienation of the library's content and founded a legacy for his heirs ordering the enlargement of the book stock. The heirs transferred the library to the Franciscans only in 1756. Nowadays some pieces of the book-collection can be found in Eisenstadt, some in Moscow, but some samples are part of different book collections in Budapest.[26]

Paul Esterházy raised also some monuments to commemorate his obtaining high-positioned posts. The monuments were erected to honor those saints who were the patrons of the day on which he was granted the post. Thus when he was elected Palatine on Saint Anton's day, he ordered a monument to Saint Anton to be raised on the court of

---

[21] Katona Imre, *A fraknói kincstár 1725-ös leltára,* "Művészettörténeti Értesítő" (1980) 2, pp. 131–147; *idem, A fraknói kincstár 1685. évi leltára,* "Savaria. A Vas megyei múzeumok értesítője" (1983/84) 17/18, pp. 461–502.

[22] The treasury was presented in a lively description by Simon Meller. Meller Simon, *Az Esterházy képtár története,* Budapest 1915, p. 21.

[23] Barkóczy (quot. nr. 2), pp. 175–177.

[24] Zimányi Vera, *Die Hofhaltung und Lebensweise der Esterházy im 17. Jahrhundert,* [in:] *Von Bildern und anderen Schätzen...,* pp. 257–276, in this case p. 266.

[25] Monok István, *Esterházy Pál könyvtára és olvasmányai,* [in:] *Arisztokrácia, Művészetek, Mecenatúra...,* pp. 91–102, in this case p. 94.

[26] Monok (quot. nr. 24), p. 91.

his Forchtenstein Castle or when he got the title of the Prince he ordered a Saint Mathias statue to be carved in Kismarton (today Eisenstadt, Austria).[27]

The Precious Pálffy Movables

Besides the Esterházy family whose members laid the economic basis of the family by their successful marriages, another family, the Pálffy started to obtain donations from the King for their fighting against the Turks.

In the testament made by Palatine Paul Pálffy in 1653 it is possible to read that a golden cup and his father's sword that he fought with against the Turks would always form part of the family fideicommissum which has to be inherited always by the senior member of the family.[28]

The history of the cup is interesting. It has inspired many historians and art historians over the last two centuries. It was Nicholaus Pálffy who obtained the cup from the estates of the realm of the province of Lower-Austria when he distinguished himself in the battle fought in order to recapture the Castle of Győr from the Turks in 1598.[29] After this triumph, both the estates of Hungary and Lower-Austria were grateful to him. The Hungarian estates and orders remembered the valour of Nicholaus Pálffy in Act 48 of 1599 and they asked the King to reward him with a donation. King Rudolf II donated to him the perpetual lordship of Pozsony (today Bratislava, Slovak Republic) together with all the property belonging to it. The estates and orders of Lower-Austria expressed their gratitude by offering him "an artistically ornamented golden cup worth a thousand lions".[30] In 1621 this cup was given to Gábor Bethlen, Prince of Transylvania, as ransom for Stephan Pálffy who was Paul's brother and who was captured in the battle of Érsekújvár. Gabriel Bethlen gave this cup as a gift to the Turkish Sultan who then gave

---

[27] Géza Galavics, *A Mecénás Esterházy Pál (vázlat egy pályaképhez)*, "Művészettörténeti Értesítő" (1988) 3/4, pp. 136–161, in this case pp. 146–147.

[28] The Hungarian version of Paul Pálffy's testament can be found in Vienna. HHSTA. F.A. PÁLFFY Arma I. Lad. 9. Fasc III. Nr. 21. – In latin the provisions of the testament are as follows: "Idem etiam statuo de domo ac horto meo Posoniensi, idem quoque de poculo meo aureo, quod parenti meo optimae recordationis tempore recuperationis praesidii Jauriensis ob praeclara eiusdem merita obtulerat provincia Austria, quod poculum frater meus, quondam dominus comes Stephanus Pálffy in eliberationem capitis sui dederat, ac tandem in manus suae sacratissimae maiestatis devenerat, quae ex singulari sua gratia illud mihi deinde dona dedit, mandoque ut tam poculum hoc, quam domus ac. hortus posoniensis uti etiam framea piae defuncti condam parentis mei, qua in antelata recuperatione praesidii Jauriensis accingebatur, eadem modo, sicut praefata bona, in primogenitura erecta, semper apud primogenitum meum, ac reliquos deinde primogenitos permaneant." MOL, Liber Regius vol. XI, p. 38.

[29] About the heroism of Nicholaus Pálffy see Peres Zsuzsanna, *"Sei es ihm ein Pokal für seine Heldentat gegeben..." (Die Belohnung von Miklós Pálffy während des Türkenkriegs)*, [in:] *Recht ohne Grenzen. Festschrift zum 15. Jubileum der Zusammenarbeit der Grazer und Pécser Rechtshistoriker, A Pécsi Tudományegyetem Jogtörténeti Tanszékének kiadványai 10*, ed. Herger Csabáné, Korsósné Delacasse Krisztina, Szekeres Róbert, Pécs 2008, pp. 83–108.

[30] There are lots of descriptions of this cup: F. Vattai Erzsébet, *Pálffy Miklós győzelmi serlege*, [in:] "Művészet" 1966. VII. évf. 5 szám; Galavics Géza, *Kössünk kardot az pogány ellen (török háborúk és képzőművészet)*, Budapest 1986, p. 27; Ipolyi Arnold, *A Pálffy család díszserlege*, "Családi Lapok" (1856) 9. szám, pp. 389–395; Báránéné Oberschall, Magda: Pálffy Miklós aranyserlege a Magyar Történeti Múzeumban, [in:] Magyar Művészet XIV., 1938, pp. 282–285; Pulszky Károly, Radisics Jenő, *Az ötvösség remekei a magyar történeti ötvöskiállításon*, Budapest 1884.

it back to Emperor Ferdinand II when the Peace contract of Szőny was signed in 1646. Ferdinand II in his turn donated the cup back to Palatine Paul Pálffy. It became such an important relict to Paul Pálffy that he founded *fideicommissum* on it in order to keep it safe from any danger together with the sword his father had fought with.[31]

The Erdődy Treasures

The link between the Erdődy family and that of Esterházy was established when George Erdődy the younger married Therese Esterházy, the daughter of Paul Esterházy. This link affected the Erdődy family. They also began to perform the function of the patrons of art.[32] The Erdődy family, like that of Esterházy and that of Pálffy, became really important in the field of politics from the 17th century on. The Erdődy's roots reached back to the most famous Hungarian clerical person Thomas Bakócz. In 1511 Wladislaw II donated the title of Count to the members of the family, whose title was strengthened in 1565. On this occasion Peter Erdődy and his children Thomas, Peter, Anna and Margaret together were granted the title of German imperial Counts.[33]

The Erdődy family was one of these families who owned a huge fideicommissum property on the territory of which is nowadays the Slovak Republic. The property was called Galgócz (today Hlohovec). This fideicommissum was founded by younger George Leopold Erdődy on the Castle of Galgócz and the property that belonged to the Castle that was donated to him by King Charles III. A very valuable treasury belonged to this fideicommissum. The research on the Erdődy family's documents showed that the treasury existed as early as the time when George Leopold Erdődy obtained Galgócz and according to the testament of George Erdődy, the senior, who was the Lord Chief Justice of the King's Court in 1713, it had to be inherited indivisible, its alienation being forbidden. In the 18th century, as a result of the *defectus seminis* in the family the immovable and movable fideicommissum property was cumulated in the hand of the same heir.

George Erdődy the senior was the Lord-Lieutenant of more counties (Árva, Bars, Sáros and Varasd among others). His first wife was Elisabeth Rákóczi who was also titulated as "Diana of Kistapolcsány" for the pleasure she found in hunting and writing poems. During her life Elisabeth Rákóczi met Paul Esterházy, they became friends and the Palatine was that person who stood beside her when she sued her husband for separation and demanded the ownership of her property. Following the example of Paul Esterházy, Elisabeth Rákóczi raised an epitaph for her former husband Adam Erdődy who died in the battle of Szászlónya. Similarly to Paul Esterházy she also founded a shrine on her property in Kistapolcsány. As owner of more goldsmith's and silversmith's artworks and jewels that she brought from the Rákóczi family she carefully prepared several inventories herself. On the bases of these inventories the art historians can reconstruct

---

[31] Jedlicska Pál, *Eredeti részletek Gróf Pálffy – család okmánytárához 1401–1653 s gróf Pálffyak életrajzi vázlatai*, Budapest 1910, p. 36.

[32] Bubryák Orsolya, *Az ősök tisztelete az Erdődy grófok mecénási programjában*, [in:] *Idővel paloták ... Magyar udvari kultúra a 16–17. században*, ed. G. Etényi Nóra, Horn Ildikó, Budapest 2005, pp. 549–581, in this case p. 554.

[33] Benda Borbála, *Az Erdődy család 17. századi genealógiája*, "Turul" 2007/(80 évf.) 4, pp. 109–125, in this case p. 111.

the list of those movables that originated from the Rákóczi family.[34] Unfortunately she died in 1707 without any heirs, so all her property was inherited by her husband George Erdődy who at that time married Therese Jakusith of Orbova. This marriage also remained childless so the fortune devolved to Christopher Erdődy's sons, Christopher being George Erdődy's brother. The fideicommissum created by George Erdődy[35] on his precious movables passed to Leslie Adam Erdődy, the bishop of Nyitra, first and at his death it was inherited by George Leopold Erdődy the younger who incorporated it into the Galgócz fideicommmissum.

According to the inventories of the 18th century the Erdődy family owned hundreds of paintings and an immense collection of guns, porcelains and goblins but because of the untimely and not-detailed descriptions they cannot be identified nowadays precisely.

Even though the above mentioned collections were not preserved in their integrity they nevertheless, when seen in the Budapest museums, are formative of our idea on the richness of the Hungarian aristocratic families that accumulated their fortunes from the 17th century on. On that occasion the legal historian may conclude that, apart from its weak points, the fideicomissum served good purpose, too.

The Cultural Heritage of the Hungarian Fideicommissa

Summary

This article discusses the way in which there were preserved until our time the precious movables of the famous Hungarian aristocratic families like those of the Esterházy, Pálffy and Erdődy that arrived at their importance during the 17th and the beginning of the 18th centuries. Thanks to the spreading of the Baroque and the appearance of the concept of the fideicommissum which was adopted in the Act 9 of 1687 these movables could be preserved in their integrity and at present they form a part of the permanent collections of different Hungarian Museums. The counter-reformation and the Baroque were the catalysers of the tendency toward the artistic patronage among the Hungarian nobles. The tendency was also exponential of their religious devotion toward the Roman Catholic Church. The devotion was materialized in the creation of several pious and charitable foundations and legacies. The nobles collected works of art and started to reconstruct their family-trees. Fideicommissum was the institution that contributed to the conservation of these collections by restraining the right of their alienation and eliminating their subjection to encumbrances.

The noble families exploited the Baroque style to rise their prestige and to form a new style of life.

---

[34] Bubryák Orsolya, *Egy 17. századi nemesasszony inventáriumai. Adatok Rákóczy Erzsébet tárházához,* "Művészettörténeti Értesítő" (2005) LIV. /1–2. pp. 41–71, in this case pp. 55–63.

[35] The original testament can be found in Vienna. HHStA F.A. Erdődy Lad. 3. Fasc. 4. Nr. 10.

WŁADYSŁAW PĘKSA

The Hungarian Feudal Institutions as Found in the Legal System of the Second Polish Republic. The Relationships between the Estate Manor and the Village in the Polish Spisz (Szepes) and Polish Orawa (Arva)

1. Geographical Limits of the Discussed Problem

When, following World War II, Poland restored her independence the Polish-Czechoslovakian borderline resembled to a large extent the former borderline between Austria and Prussia as well as the borderline that at one time divided Cislitavia (Cisleithanien) and Translitavia (Transleithanien) in the former Austro-Hungarian monarchy. In some small areas the aforementioned borderline was subjected to changes which the ethnic relationships or political reasons necessitated. The changes of that type were detectable in the area of Spisz (Szepes) and Orawa (Arva). In this territory the borderline was shifted to the south. As a result two small parts of the previous territory of Hungarian Kingdom (in its shape from 1917/1918) found themselves within the boundaries of Poland.[1] The Hungarian law remained in force in this area in compliance with the time-sanctified principle which commanded to respect the law which previously governed this region.

On that occasion it is worthwhile to emphasize that the discussed part of the former Hungarian Sepesz territory which belonged to Poland from 1918 was quite different from the area of the Zips pledge of the 15th through 18th centuries.[2]

---

[1] J. Bardach, B. Leśnodorski, M. Pietrzak, *Historia ustroju i prawa polskiego*, Warszawa 1999, pp. 465–467.

[2] In exchange for a loan of sixty times the amount of 37,000 Prague groschen, that is approximately seven tons of pure silver, the Hungarian crown pawned 16 rich salt-producing towns in the area of Spisz (Zips), as well as the right to incorporate them into Poland until the debt is repaid. The debt was not repaid and the area of Spisz remained a part of Poland until the partitions of Poland in the late 18th century. In 1769, during the Bar Confederation, the Austrian forces of Joseph II, Holy Roman Emperor, acting under the pretext of securing the region from war took control of the towns. See more about Zips pledge: "strona główna": http://en.wikipedia.org/wiki/Treaty_of_Lubowla [acceded: 15.07.2009]. Available in internet http://en.wikipedia.org/w/index.php?title=Treaty_of_Lubowla&action=edit§ion=1.

2. The Time Limits within which the Hungarian Law Remained in Force in the Territory of the Second Republic of Poland

Prior to the unification of her civil law, Poland of the inter war time was subject to five legal systems including, among others, that of Germany (the BGB), that of Austria (the ABGB), that of Russia, that of Hungary and that of France. The French law governed for instance the civil law relationships in the former Congress Kingdom since the Napoleonic Code Civil survived there in its amended form. The eastern part of the country was subject to Russian civil law of Svod Zakonov in its 20th century version. In the early 1920s, and specifically in 1921 and 1922, the Austrian ABGB acquired its binding force in the Polish Spisz and Orawa. Among the exceptions that were made with regard to this territory was the Hungarian law of succession which was left intact. In that respect the last remnants of Hungarian legal system were repealed only after World War II on occasion of abolishing the Hungarian law of succession. This was done by the Statute of 8 Oct. 1946.[3]

It is worthwhile to note that during the inter-war period Poland made a considerable effort to produce modern national codifications in various legal branches (in civil and penal substantive law, the procedures etc.) but this codification process was not completed before the outbreak of World War II. [4]

3. The Hungarian Legal Remnants

What was binding in Spisz and Orawa was the survival of certain customary norms of the Hungarian law. These norms regulated the serfdom–like relationships that linked the owner of the manorial estate and the peasants who were the inhabitants of three villages in Spisz: Falsztyn (Falstin), Łapsze (Alsólápos, Felsőlápos) and Niedzica (Nedec). These serfdom-like relationships resembled those prevalent in Galicia (Galizien being the Polish province of Cisleithanien) in the 19th century prior to the 1848 agrarian reform that abolished the feudal services. The aforementioned peasants were obliged to work the manorial estate, i.e. to render the services resembling those of the serf labour type. They were expected to do it in exchange for their right to have in possession a piece of land and the house that was formally owned by the landlord.

That kind of semi-serfdom relationships survived in the discussed area until the Statute of the 20th of March 1931[5] when, under the pressure of the peasant political parties, these relationships were abolished.[6] It is interesting to find that the discussed relationships between the landlord and the peasants were refered to as the *żeleri* relationships

---

[3] Statute of 8 October, 1946 ("Journal of Laws", No. 46, 1946, item 329).

[4] S. Płaza, *Historia prawa w Polsce na tle porównawczym*, t. III, Cracow/Kraków 2001, pp. 34–35, also: J. Ciągwa, *Recepcja prawa węgierskiego na Spiszu i Orawie po 1920 r.*, "Studia Historyczne", nr 39, 1996.

[5] Statute of 20 March 1931 on the liquidation of the *żeleri* relationships in Spisz, ("Journal of Laws", 1931, No 037, item 289).

[6] F. Gwiżdż, *Polski słownik biograficzny*, Ossolineum 1960, vol. IX/1, z. 40 (Feliks Gwiżdż was one of the peasant politicians who prepared the abolishing of the *żeleri* relationships).

(in Polish: *stosunki żelarskie)*, the peasants themselves being called *żeleri* which was typical Hungarian terminology.

The survival of this kind of semi-feudal relationships in Spisz and Orawa aroused a considerable interest among the Polish anthropologists, sociologists and historians. The phenomenon was studied as a kind of the "living fossils" resembling that of *latimeria*: the fish from prehistoric era that is still detectable in some regions. The *żeleris* were interviewed by the scholars almost like the Indians in the reserve that should be preserved since they made up a kind of curiosity.[7]

The Polish Ministry of Agriculture of inter war time tried to arrive at a deep insight into the matter.[8] Its staff asked therefore Oskar Balzer, a renown Polish legal historian, for his opinion. Balzer made it clear that the Hungarian law of the early 20th century could not provide the basis for the specific relationships that linked the landlord and the peasants in Spisz and Orawa. He emphasized the fact that the Hungarian Constitution of 1848 abolished serfdom and peasant services previously rendered to the owners of manorial estates. What therefore might account for the specific relationships detectable in Spisz and Orawa would be justified only on the basis of civil law contract. On the other hand Balzer found that the peasants could not confirm their duties by any written contract. At the same time their status was considered hereditary. Also the number of days during which they were obliged to render their services to the manor resembled that typical of the Theresian *urbarium* of the 18th century.[9]

The researchers who tried to elucidate the situation used to conclude that there were the economic and social reasons rather then legal which were responsible for the survival of the unique arrangements that bound the peasants and their landlord. The *żeleri* who resembled the serfs were the inhabitants of remote isolated villages which, in the circumstances of heavy winter, were hardly accessible and are hardly accessible even today. The level of cultural development of the inhabitants was rather low (most of them were illiterate). The tradition had it that the heads of peasant families were responsible for the services that all family members were expected to render. On the part of the landlord these were his officials who represented him. There were two landlord families that came into play: Salomon family who were of Hungarian extraction and who owned the Niedzica estate (Nedec-Vár estate), and the Jungenfeld family who were the owners of Falsztyn and who represented the Hungarian nobility of German origin.[10]

In the discussed relationships the routine that was followed consisted in the landlord securing the land, the house or the building material as well as the right to use the forest to a specific żelari family. In addition, he guaranteed the family a kind of protection. In

---

[7] M. Hulewiczowa, *Pozostałości ustroju pańszczyźnianego w XX wieku na polskim Spiszu i Orawie*, "Roczniki Dziejów Społecznych i Gospodarczych" (Annales D'Histoire Sociale et Economique), vol. VII, 1938, Lwów (Lemberg), pp. 107–134.

[8] *Umowa między wyżej podpisanemi stronami względem plebańskich zysków parafii jabłońskiej (…)* preserved in Nowy Targ Starostwo (county) Archive. Appendix in "Roczniki Dziejów Społecznych i Gospodarczych" (Annales D'Histoire Sociale et Economique), vol. VII, 1938, Lwów (Lemberg), pp. 137–139.

[9] *Prof. O.Balcer's opinion (Opinia prof. Oswalda Balzera o żelarstwie na Spiszu)* preserved in Nowy Targ Starostwo (county) Archive. Case IIIf, No. 22, also: Appendix in "Roczniki Dziejów Społecznych i Gospodarczych" (Annales D'Histoire Sociale et Economique), vol. VII, 1938, Lwów (Lemberg), pp. 134ff.

[10] A. Kroh, *Spisz, Spis, Zips, Szepesz*, [in:] *Spisz, wielokulturowe dziedzictwo*, Sejny 2000, pp. 9–24; M. Liptak, *Kim są Niemcy spiscy (karpaccy)*, [in:] *ibidem*, pp. 31–37.

return for that the peasant family was required to render the labour that varied from 56 to 100 days per year for one "morga" (piece of land equal to 6578 square yards).

Each peasant could theoretically resign from rendering the services in question but that would mean that he would have to leave the land and the house which many generations of his family previously occupied. On the other hand the peasants treated the land they occupied as their hereditary possession. Also if one of the family members left for America to earn money to improve his position other individuals of the family used to render the services instead of him. Likewise, according to the Hungarian law of 1896 if the *żelari* decided to refuse rendering the discussed services the landlord could demand that such peasant should compulsorily buy the previously occupied land. But the terms of such transaction were so unfavourable to the peasant that there would hardly be anyone determined to conclude such a contract.

When in 1926 the *żelari* of Falsztyn village refused to render their services to the landlord the latter filed a suit in the Court of Nowy Sącz against them.[11] The Court however dismissed the suit while arguing that since the 1921 and 1922 Statutes the Hungarian law no longer remained in force. The landlord lodged the appeal from this decision with the Cracow [Appeal] Court but without any success. It was also one of the last cases of applying Hungarian law by the courts on that area.[12]

Let us emphasize that the *żelari* were the minority among the population of the village in which they lived. Most of the peasants were free of the duties to which the *żelari* were subject. The *żelari* were poor and non-educated, and occupied the lowest position in social stratification. It is until now that in the local Polish patois the noun *żelari* smuggles a pejorative tone.[13]

The Hungarian Feudal Institutions as Found in the Legal System of the Second Polish Republic. The Relationships between the Estate Manor and the Village in the Polish Spisz (Szepes) and Polish Orawa (Arva)

Summary

The present paper discusses the unique customary norms of Hungarian law that until the 1920s survived within the boundaries of Poland in the area that at one time was a part of the Hungarian Crown. The discussed norms regulated the relationships between the landlord-controlled manor and the peasants inhabitting the area. The norms were found to be reflective of serfdom services that at one time the peasants were required to render for the benefit of the owner of the landed estate.

---

[11] Before 1918 that area was subjected to the Court of Spiska Nova Ves (Igló, Zipser Neuendorf).
[12] Hulewiczowa, pp. 122.
[13] *Ibidem*, pp. 124ff.

TECHNICAL EDITOR

Renata Włodek

PROOFREADER

Marta Janiszewska-Hanusiak

TYPESETTER

Katarzyna Mróz

Jagiellonian University Press
ul. Michałowskiego 9/2, 31-126 Kraków
Phone: 12-631-18-81, Phone: 12-631 18 82, Fax: 12-631-18-83